The authors

bring a ~~~~~~ ~~~~~~~ experience to support the ideas they put forward in this book. They know the world. Between them they have visited and worked in 89 countries in every continent, and have dwelt for extended periods in ten of those. They have been involved in development issues over the last twenty-five years, and have written extensively on the topic. They have been responsible for the development of a bio-physical modelling procedure known as natural capital accounting which has taken root in several institutes. They are both founder members of the International Network of Resource Information Centers, more commonly known as the Balaton Group.

MALCOLM SLESSER graduated in chemical engineering and worked in the oil, synthetic fibres and nuclear industries before taking up a post at Strathclyde University, where he eventually became Professor of Energy Studies. He has taught in the USA and Brazil, and was for three years head of systems analysis with the European Commission in Italy. He retired to an honorary position at Edinburgh University in 1981 and for seventeen years led a research team in natural capital accounting, fulfilling many contracts with the aid of post-graduate students and assistants from all over the world. He is currently chairman of the Resource Use Institute. He has published ten books, over thirty refereed papers and many articles. He is a well-known mountaineer and arctic explorer.

JANE KING left Moscow and the diplomatic service to work with the new International Institute for Educational Planning in Paris. From there she was appointed to head human resources planning in Mauritius in the lead up to the island's independence. She has always been fascinated by the non-economic, longer-term factors affecting economic development and moved back to Paris and to Unesco where she took responsibility for working out new approaches to assessing the relationship between population and development. In that role she became active in wider United Nations' efforts to identify the ways in which population and natural resources affect a nation's development prospects – the precursor of current concerns about sustainable development. Within that programme she played a leading part in devising the new methodology for quantifying population/resource/environment interactions known as natural capital accounting, and in testing it with the collaboration of several national teams. In 1986, in order to concentrate on this approach she moved home to Scotland, becoming an honorary fellow at the University of Edinburgh. She has many publications to her credit and speaks several languages.

OTHER BOOKS BY MALCOLM SLESSER INCLUDE:

Brazil: Land Without Limit, Allen and Unwin, 1969
The Politics of the Environment, Allen and Unwin, 1972
Energy in the Economy, Macmillan, 1978
Biological Energy Resources (with C. Lewis), Spon, 1979
Dictionary of Energy, Macmillan, 1982, 1988
GlobEcco Manual, RUI Publishing, 1995
UKEcco, RUI Publishing, 1996
The Management of Greed (with D.C. Crane and J. King), RUI Publishing, 1997
RegEcco Manual, RUI Publishing, 1998

OTHER BOOKS BY JANE KING INCLUDE:

Planning Non-formal Education in Tanzania, Unesco, 1967
Beyond Economic Choice: Population and Sustainable Development, 1987, University of Edinburgh in association with UNESCO

Not by Money Alone

Economics as nature intended

Malcolm Slesser & Jane King

JON CARPENTER

Our books may be ordered from bookshops or (post free) from
Jon Carpenter Publishing at the address below

Credit card orders should be phoned or faxed to 01689 870437
or 01608 811969

First published in 2002 by
Jon Carpenter Publishing
Alder House, Market Street, Charlbury, Oxfordshire OX7 3PH
☎ 01608 811969

ISBN 1 897766 72 6

Printed in England by Antony Rowe Ltd., Chippenham

Contents

Acknowledgements

One can only add new bricks to an old wall if the foundations are secure. In writing this book we have been lucky in being able to draw on an immense variety of solid information from colleagues. To change the metaphor, the recipe is ours, but the pudding could never have been made without their contributions.

Those whose work we have quoted, borrowed or pillaged are too numerous to mention, but there are three who cannot be omitted. The first is Dr. Anupam Saraph who directs the Institute for Change Research in Goa, India. Many years ago with his brilliant help we developed a bio-physical computer model of the world. Extracts have been used to illustrate some of the issues discussed in this book. The second is Dr. David Cooper Crane, who worked with us for many years further developing models of the UK, Scotland and Europe. He undertook the enormous task of preparing the technical manuals which explain every aspect of these models. The third is in the plural: the many far flung members of the Balaton Group, otherwise known as the International Network of Resource Information Centers (INRIC). Their many and varied contributions to the issues pertaining to sustainability provided an immense intellectual store that we have mined in preparing this book.

Finally, we have to thank Jon Carpenter for his painstaking perusal of the manuscript and many helpful suggestions.

Jane King and Malcolm Slesser

Glossary

Anaerobic Digestion or decay occurring in the absence of oxygen.

Available capacity The capacity available, as opposed to the potential. See load factor and capacity.

BAU Business-as-usual – the proposition that all existing policies continue indefinitely into the future. Usually used as a reference against which other policies may be judged.

Biomass Anything grown; but more specifically, carbon-containing products which when dry can be burnt to release energy.

Capacity In the sense of power, the potential to produce output at 100% load factor (q.v.).

Carrying capacity Used in this book in the sense of the population that can be supported from indigenous resources at a given material standard of living.

CO_2 The gas carbon dioxide. It is a greenhouse gas.

Depletable resource A resource which cannot be renewed within a meaningful time scale, such as fossil fuels.

E-commerce Trading on the Internet.

EU European Union, which currently (2002) comprises 15 countries.

Fuel An energy source in a form ready for application – to be distinguished from primary energy which needs refining before it can be applied.

G Abbreviation for giga – a billion (= thousand million).

GJ Billion joules – common scientific unit of energy.

G-7 Shorthand for the seven most economically influential countries: USA, UK, France, Germany, Canada, Japan and Italy. With Russia it is known as G-8.

Greenhouse gas A gas that traps infra-red radiation from Earth out to space, thus warming the atmosphere.

GDP Gross Domestic Product – a monetary measure of national output.

HMC Human made (i.e. manufactured) capital, to distinguish it from natural capital (q.v.).

Hedge fund A fund whose objective is to hedge against financial uncertainty.

IMF International Monetary Fund.

Joule An internationally accepted and defined unit of energy. The energy conveyed by one watt of power for one second.

kWh (kilowatt-hour) The energy conveyed by a power source of one kilowatt for one hour. In this book units of watts such as Kilowatts, (kW), Megawatts (MW) etc. only apply to electricity and its generation.

Load factor Averaged over a period of time such as a year, the proportion of power capacity that is actually utilised.

Long term In this book long term would be considered 10 years or more

M (Mega) = million.

MJ Million joules.

Mental model One's perception of how something works.

Model Used here in the sense of a computer model, that is the mathematical description of a system of inter-locking factors.

Natural capital Anything physical pertaining to the Earth or its atmosphere.

PJ (Peta-joule) A million million joules.

Phlogiston An imaginary element of negative weight that at one time was used to explain the weight change that took place when burning a fuel.

Resource A form of natural capital that can be exploited with current technology at present prices.

Reserve A potential resource probably accessible if new technology develops or if prices of currently available resources rise.

Scenario A visualisation of the future, usually in the context of proposed policies or likely trends.

SO$_2$ The gas sulphur dioxide.

Souming A share – see Chapter 8.

Thermodynamics The science of the relationships between heat and *work*.

Tonne Metric tonne, 1000 kilograms. 10% greater than an imperial ton.

Tonne oil equivalent (TOE) The heat that can be released on combusting one tonne of oil. Since oil is a mixture of many hydrocarbons by convention a TOE is taken to be 41.8 GJ.

Work The *work* in a scientific sense done when something is moved or transformed. In this book it is always expressed in italics to distinguish it from work in the social sense.

Foreword

BY AUBREY MANNING

For an increasing number of us, there regularly comes the uncomfortable recognition that the current way we run our national and international affairs cannot survive for much longer. We still measure economic health in terms of how much we consume, receiving almost weekly anxious updates on how 'high street spending' is going. At the same time we are aware of gross disparities between the prosperity of rich and poor nations, disparities which are increasing at a time when the rich nations worry if their economic growth rate even shows the least sign of faltering. This growth rate requires ever increasing supplies of cheap energy whose consumption is beginning to have global effects on climate which can no longer be ignored.

We urgently need some radical and lateral thinking, which is at the same time realistic, taking off with the argument from the point at which we stand with all the attitudes that inhibit change. I believe we have it with this book. Slesser and King both have broad and varied experience in politics, economics and the environmental sciences. They have recently been much concerned in developing systems of 'Natural Capital Accounting', assessing the interactions between a nation's natural resources and its population with their requirements and expectations.

Here they develop in an attractive way many ideas of how we could break free of the current economic obsessions – which will destroy us in the long run – to develop an economy that reflects the natural, ecological constraints. Rightly they concentrate on energy supplies and how we might conserve them through a totally new approach to taxation. Their style is lively and irreverent; they never preach, although they are not afraid to point out the moral issues involved in moving towards sustainable societies – 'durable' is the term they prefer. Above all they examine in practical and informed ways *how* we can move forward. This is a positive and optimistic book, for though they understand clearly which technological changes are not going to be possible, equally clearly they indicate which aspects of human attitude and ingenuity (with attendant huge opportunities for economic activity) will help. It ought to be compulsory reading in Whitehall and Brussels, but there is something in it for all of us.

Preface

Two decades ago a term was coined which seemed to offer a new hope: sustainable development. It suggested a future in which people would live in harmony with nature: where the bounties she bestows upon us would be wisely husbanded and the waste products of human activity kept to a rate that the environment could cope with. And in that future a balance would be maintained between the size of populations and the natural resources available. The physical needs of each one of us could be met and the potential created for all to live meaningful lives.

Sadly, the human race has not proved wise enough to turn hope into reality. We have been lured by consumerism and the material promises of globalisation away from the fact that sooner or later, if we take no action, nature will exact a heavy price for the depredations we are inflicting upon her. The meaning of *sustainability* has been so degraded, so trivialised, that the original message has all but disappeared and with it the sense of urgency it once implied. Instead we are offered pious platitudes, often couched in empty jargon. Politicians, corporate leaders, environmentalists and the media: they are all at it. It is a fair bet that someone is spouting about *sustainable development* in a place near you at this very moment.

Now, this is said without wishing to dispute the good intentions of those who utter this mantra with such frequency and gravity. Achieving sustainability, though, is not just a matter of trimming the sails in a freshening breeze till we reach a safe haven: a bit of energy efficiency here, some waste recycling there. The truth is that a gale is in the offing and it will require some astute handling to steer the ship to safety.

How is it that this is not apparent to all? The reason is that we have fallen into the trap of thinking that everything can be reduced to money, overlooking the fact that what is not physically feasible can never be economically possible.

In this book we seek to demonstrate why money cannot encompass nature, and that if we wish to sail our ship along a course towards durable development we have to work things out on her terms, using science not economics. This means becoming more aware of the primary, indeed defining, role of energy in our affairs, and the fact that we are living off an inheritance of finite energy resources at an extraordinary rate – as if we believed there will be no tomorrow.

Of course every reader knows that we cannot live by money alone. In this book we appeal not only to altruism but to reason. In Chapter 1 we explain why money cannot be used to assess sustainability in the true sense of durability. In Chapter 2 we demonstrate why energy has to be brought into the calculus.

But money and energy are not the only determinants. What makes the world controllable, in its biological, physical and financial aspects, is the principle of feedback, one of whose commonest manifestations is the free market mechanism of supply and demand. The principles of positive and negative feedback need to be well comprehended, especially by legislators. This is the topic of Chapter 3.

The curious reader will want to know more about the money argument than is offered in Chapter 1. In Chapter 4 we explore in depth the meaning of money, and find that what it really measures is human decision. And that being so, we then need to find new ways in which the environment can be incorporated into economic analysis. This is the stuff of Chapter 5.

Now nature's resources are highly varied, but they tend to fall into three broad types: depletable, recyclable and renewable. They are collectively known as natural capital to distinguish them from human-made capital. Clearly if energy resources are indeed finite the reader deserves to be put in the picture, and this we do in Chapter 6, including a discussion of prospects for the future. A further valuable contribution of nature is the absorption of humanly generated wastes. This is so important that the whole of Chapter 7 is devoted to it.

From Chapter 8 onwards we're trying to find solutions: that passage to a safe haven. Being of a concerned disposition, like our readers, we believe that the global commons have to be shared, and we put forward an idea or two on that score. To meet that objective a workable mechanism has to be established within our societies, so we offer in Chapter 9 some taxation ideas that hook neatly into the principles of the free market.

Without vision, of course, we will never embark on this voyage of discovery. But we need caution and common sense as well. It is easy to imagine that with modern technology, new ideas and careful planning, durable development is already in the bag. We test out the situation in Chapter 10 using a resource-based model of the European Union, and find that it is very, very difficult to meet all desired objectives: physical, social, economic and political. This is a cautionary tale, and no doubt some other parts of the world will be better placed. Finally we indulge in moralising a little in Chapter 11 on the world we deserve, and put forward some ideas whereby that bogeyman institution, the World Trade Organisation, may be re-jigged to help attain the durable economy and environment that so many dream about.

Malcolm Slesser and Jane King, Edinburgh, July 2001

1

Not by money alone ...

Am fear as fhaide a bhios beo 'se a chi toradh na h-obrach seo.
(*The man that lives longest will see what comes of work of this kind.*)
GAELIC SAYING

If you are in peril of your life, say in the path of an impending tidal wave, your instinct is to save yourself. The underlying physics of the event will be far from your thoughts. It is only later, safe and mentally restored, that you might dwell intellectually upon the forces underlying the event.

The situation that we, the peoples of the world, find ourselves in today is not so different. Nature seems to be hurling at us more than the usual number of hurricanes, floods and so forth which, with the increase in population density, has resulted in huge loss of life and property. It appears that we are in a period of global warming of our own human making, which will occasion all sorts of uncertain events. We are enjoined by our governments to cut back on fossil fuel use as burning it creates carbon dioxide, reckoned to be one of the causes of this new risk. On top of that we find that our agriculture seems not to be capable of bringing us safe food. We can no longer escape the inference that our own economic activities and the density of our population are factors in all these trends.

Problems like these cannot be solved by throwing money at them. What indeed does nature care for money? We need rather to apply science to understand not only what is happening in the natural world as a result of our activities, but how far and in what manner we can ensure that our economic development be compatible with environmental laws.

Already a devoted few, aware of the dangers, have chosen to deprive themselves of material luxuries in order to help 'save the planet'. The sad fact is that they are considered an irrelevance by the wider world. A way forward cannot be achieved by the abnegation of a minority. They may be admired but rarely emulated. The solution must be through a wider understanding by the public at large of the limitations and opportunities provided by the natural world. Here we need science more than economics.

We shall demonstrate in this book that it is quite possible to bring about a seamless evolution from today's frenetic fossil-based, energy-intensive economy to one that can be both sustainable and environmentally benign as well as materially abundant. Being Green, as it were, does not mean having to be deprived of modern amenities, but it does mean taking firm steps in the right direction.

Unfortunately some of the propositions of the environmentalists and Green parties are frankly untenable. To give an example, Greenpeace, a most worthy environmental organisation, claims that there is no need to exploit the oil frontier west of Shetland: that the UK could, if its government had the will, move directly to an economy driven by renewable energies and still remain materially comfortable. Alas, the issue is not so simple. We shall need decades of investment and all the oil we can get to effect the transition from a fossil (and fissile) based energy economy to one driven by renewable energy, for the simple fact that to build the alternative systems requires the expenditure of much energy. Later we shall explain exactly how we come to that conclusion.

This is not to suggest that the world economy is about to run down, with even those who can afford it (and many cannot) no longer able to heat their houses, run their cars or enjoy clean drinking water. But it could happen if we, as a civilisation, do not take the trouble to re-locate our thinking within nature. A stumbling block is that almost all decision-making is today enumerated in monetary terms, which excludes nature. This is what we have to change, and to do so we have to embark on an intellectual journey which will undermine much conventional thinking.

Money is perceived as the key that unlocks the door to opportunity and choice. It is the flux by which the economy operates. Small wonder then that many have devoted their lives to its pursuit, unaware of the fact that money has no intrinsic value of its own. The truth is that while those who have it are able to acquire a greater share of the economic pie, money is no more than a veil draped over the physical asset upon which we all depend, obscuring the nature of the real world.

It would be another matter if the physical asset were endlessly abundant in its support of human activity, but it seems not. This much has come to be accepted at government level in most countries. Thus does the word 'sustainability' echo frequently from the lips of politicians. Why else does it crop up so often in the grave utterances at corporate AGMs, and pepper the pages of the publications of climatologists and ecologists? Why, though, and this is the strange thing, does nobody work out scientifically the physical implications of the message the word conveys?

By physical asset we mean of course the biosphere. Efforts are often made to quantify this contribution of the environment in monetary units. Such numbers, however, have little meaning, money being what it is: a human artefact, infinitely expandable. They cannot help us to answer such a question as 'how can we create a sustainable economy when the environment is becoming overloaded and when key resources are limited?' Why they cannot will be clear, we hope, by the time you have reached the end of this book.

The physical reality lying beneath the veil is, then, the natural world: our prop and stay, the source of our raw materials, the sink that absorbs our wastes, and the source of that essential force, energy, without which no transformation, no production can occur. In this book we shall endeavour to show that if we want to look into the future to judge the options we have for developing a sustainable economy and environment, then we must do so in energetic, not monetary terms.

The fundamental problem with money is that it does not exist. It is no more than a clever invention, an abstraction. As a unit of measurement it has no absolute value, no measurable equivalent like that of length or weight. Its value is instantaneous, no more fixed than a meteor passing through the earth's orbit. It is constantly changing and no-one can foresee with any accuracy what monetary value something may have in one, ten, twenty or thirty years ahead.

In spite of this uncertainty it is common practice to measure the wealth of a country in monetary units, and use money to project the future cost of an enterprise; it is even used to value an environmental asset – a beautiful piece of countryside, say, or the ozone layer. The fact that these enumerations gain any credence is a triumph of hope over experience. But it is indefensible to use such a chimera as the basis for managing our economies in this time of stress when their maintenance, indeed durability, is entirely dependent on a sustained flow of one single, unique, physical, non-renewable, finite and therefore declining resource – namely fossil and fissile energy – and when the health of our population depends on the biosphere being able to absorb our ever-expanding stream of wastes.

The unreliability of money is not an issue that seems to have bothered our leaders, or impinged upon the thinking of vast cohorts of economists for whom money serves as the unit of account. Certainly here and there one comes across expressions of unease, and many of us frequently wonder why certain things are declared impossible because of monetary limitations when it is perfectly obvious that they are physically and socially feasible and that surplus human effort is available to manage them. But the sanctity of money is deeply embedded in our culture to the point where most of us have been brought up to think of it as a real, tangible commodity deserving protection. The possibility that some person or corporation might become monetarily poorer as a result of a decision that is morally, socially or environmentally desirable is usually enough to put an end to any greater enlightenment.

The innate trust we have in money imposes on us a false perspective of the future. For the ordinary citizen, to whom this book is addressed, there is the sensation of being trapped in a mental labyrinth. In whom and in what are we to believe and what action, in any case, can we take? It is for this reason that we must seek to understand what really underlies the economic system. We are not talking here about the driving force of human greed, but what enables that force to achieve its ends. In other words, we need to gain an understanding of the science of sustainability. The economics we know well enough. If this understanding can be brought to the electorate then, in response to popular demand, governments can probe the boundaries of what the future is physically able to offer and resolve logically some of the burning environmental issues of our times. For example, can we do without nuclear energy? Can renewable energy sufficiently replace fossil and fissile fuels to sustain our present life-styles? Will the need to maintain the environment slow down economic growth and thus cause further unemployment? Can the developing nations attain the material standards of the industrialised countries? And, most pressing of all, how does *sustainable development*, the recurrent catch phrase of our times, fit in? We cannot delay, for the hurricane of a money-based economic globalisation is tearing us from our roots. Some even say resistance is useless. The cynical advice is to adapt, to look out for yourself, and to hell with the rest. Make money as fast as you can. But to what end is making money if the system around you is collapsing?

Such exhortations must be rejected, for they surely lie on the path to social destruction. This is no David versus Goliath battle, for where is the Goliath? The trans-national companies upon whom many would heap the blame are simply responding to the exigencies of the monetary system. It is not them, but rather the system within which they operate that we have to change.

The forces of globalisation are not managed by bad people, simply by people whose perspective on life is mediated through money. Many of them worry too. They know as well as the rest of us that, to paraphrase God's words to Moses, Man does not live by money alone. It is a mistake to assume that politicians, economic experts, bankers and multinational corporations understand the economy any more than the majority of citizens.

The business decision-makers, the movers and shakers, are indeed very good at what they do. They have their eyes on the ball and the ball is profit. The only signal they recognise, though, is price. For most the long-term future is of no concern, nor can it be for money does not lend itself to prediction. '*Sufficient unto the day is the evil thereof*'. They have just one guiding principle: let the market be free. Led by the nose of this current dogma, all else follows.

Now the validity of the free market concept is based on the principle of self-

correction or, to express it more scientifically, the principle of feedback. This principle itself is entirely sound, and will be discussed in Chapter 3. In the short term
the money system deals quite well with supply and demand. If scarcity raises
prices, demand is held to fall and vice versa. The Achilles heel is that money
cannot take into account the contribution of the environment to our human
welfare, for nature puts no price upon her bounty. There is no feedback possible.
And if anyone is naive enough to imagine that we can buck nature or do without
her generous supply of raw materials and receptive environment without recognising the part she plays, then he or she deserves to be whisked away in the next
hurricane, economic or climatic.

To cling to the belief that money can measure the environment is the
economic equivalent of embracing the seventeenth-century phlogiston theory of
chemical combination (which required the concept of negative mass) or behaving
like some present-day mid-American school board denying the possibility of
Darwinian evolution. Money must be put in its proper place. The economist John
Maynard Keynes put his finger on it when he said that behind every politician was
an out-of-date economist.

Our thinking must widen to recognise that we humans are part of a huge
natural interacting feedback system. To imagine that we can simply go about our
lives flashing bank notes to make things right is as unrealistic as believing we can
live on Mars without a space suit. Unfortunately our psyches are deeply buried
in our religious inheritance, which we interpret as giving us mastery of the
universe. Were not God's words to Noah on leaving the Ark:

*'And the fear of you and the dread of you shall be upon every beast of the earth...into
your hand are they delivered.'* [1]

How presumptuous. Not a day passes but nature demonstrates her awesome
power, in the form of floods, cyclones, locust swarms or earthquakes.
Climatologists expect the weather to become more extreme as a result of global
warming[2]. Insurance companies have already taken that on board by raising their
premiums. But nature is not so supreme that she cannot be harmed by our activities. Already she is finding it hard to cope with the vast amount of pollution we
generate, and the increasing intensity with which we exploit the soil. The
biosphere[3] has reached a point where it can absorb no more of our wastes without
permanent harm. 'Our present course is unsustainable' announced the UN
Environment Programme in September 1999 on the launch of its *Global
Environment Outlook 2000 (GEO 2000)*.[4] Based on contributions from UN agencies,
850 individuals and 30 environmental institutes, GEO 2000 analysed both global

and regional issues. The report emphasises that *'postponing action is no longer an option'*. But where is the action?

The problem is not simply the environment. Society too has taken a beating. Little by little over the last few decades our sense of community has become diluted in an obsession with consumer choice, in what the broadcaster John Humphrys calls *consumer populism*. The free market has deemed that in the interest of that choice local loyalty and local production are irrelevant, but try saying this to French tomato growers or Scottish sheep farmers, whose very livelihood is threatened. A recent poignant headline in the Scottish agricultural press ran: 'Would the last sheep leaving please switch off the lights'. Nor is it just the rural population that can suffer. The urban masses too would lose if the husbandry of the countryside fell into abeyance, for a well tended agricultural scene is an aesthetic joy. And all this arises from a failure by politicians to make policy in the context of the whole system; to recognise that the purpose, the only justification, of an economy is that it should serve the people within and provide them with a decent durable environment. Our leaders have chosen one simple, misguided dictum in their search for solutions to social and economic problems: growth, growth and more growth, all because if you think in monetary units there is no alternative. Consider this quote from a business magazine. 'Since taking office in 1987, Federal Reserve Chairman Alan Greenspan has been known for his willingness to take quick and decisive action when confronted by a crisis. Now he has done it again. Facing the prospect of a rapidly slowing economy, a shrinking manufacturing sector, and a fast-declining stock market, Greenspan on January 3, 2001, led the Federal Open Market Committee in an aggressive half-percentage-point reduction in interest rates – a move that sent the stock market soaring'.[5] Not a hint in this comment of the effect it would have on energy use and the environment.

And so global competition gains momentum, and as it does it strangles the periphery. Mergers of enterprises have risen to dizzy heights. A recent amalgamation was valued at one hundred billion dollars. That is greater than the combined economic product of several of the smaller European countries.

The new marketeers are very clever. A plethora of pointless goods unknown to our predecessors now besiege our senses: bottled water, alcopops, robotic pets and computer games. Gucci, Dior, Nike and many others are successful companies not necessarily because of any particular merit in their products but because the marketing people have managed to sell the idea of social primacy. Even discomforts of old age like arthritis and back problems offer opportunities for market researchers to use computers to simulate the ailments of the geriatric contingent in the search for a means to sell more widely amongst them. In an economy driven by services the path to fiscal growth relies on selling need where none exists, often appealing to our emotional or spiritual shortcomings. As surely as the auto industry depends on metal and plastics, the service industries thrive on human desires.

But globalisation is not unstoppable if we, the people, fully understand its consequences. Who would have thought in early 1999 that popular resistance to genetically modified (GM) foods would have been so successful or that Monsanto would have had to back down on its terminator seeds? Common purpose in the old sense may be lacking, but the desire is still present in many individuals for something more than just material betterment. In spite of the onslaught of advertising most of us do not live by money alone.

Sustainable development

Let us go back to the phrase *sustainable development,* now part of popular speech and thought. Surely it reveals an ethic and objective purpose quite outside the dogma of market economics; the idea of working towards a different sort of world?

In economic theory, value is represented by each individual's subjective preferences for goods and services. Welfare is quantified in that curious term GNP (*gross national product* [6]). Yet this is no more than a valuation in monetary units of activities for which money is exchanged, while omitting anything that is provided at no charge, like the contribution of a mother to her children or nature's supply of mineral resources. Many a remote community that would be considered poor by monetary standards is rich in natural surroundings or in mutual help between neighbours. And if one believes, as do most politicians and economists, that the enlargement of GNP is a nation's most worthy aspiration, it is little wonder that we sense a downward spiral in the tone of our society. Remember President Clinton's election campaign. When asked what was most important of all, he said 'it's the economy, stupid'.

GNP may represent the national product in one sense, but there are two sides to a balance sheet and GNP as presently computed does not take account of what we plunder from the environment in order to generate that product. It is true that many people including many economists have become dissatisfied with GNP as a measure of development and that attempts have been made to deduct the contribution of the environment to arrive a net GNP. However the idea itself that the environment can be accounted for in monetary units remains one of the greater absurdities of environmental economics. And as we shall see shortly, there is even more to it than that.

Politicians, of course, like all individuals in their daily lives, do have purpose beyond simply staying in office. They hold power in a world that is conditioned to believe that growth in GNP is the best way of creating the income that can then be used to solve our – and their – problems. Politicians do care about sustainability in the sense of keeping the planet functioning well. Many accept that the world is facing a long-term environmental problem of colossal proportions. Why else would one hundred and sixty governments have met in the Hague in November 2000 to thrash out a global solution to the growing greenhouse gas menace and try yet again at Bonn in July 2001? The box on the next page summarises the July 2001 situation.

In fairness to politicians one should also not underestimate the problems they face in attempting to pursue economic development while at the same time nourishing the environment. Inevitably they are obliged to ride two horses at once. To really engage in serious environmental measures would create enormous headaches for them as it could well reduce the rate of economic growth. After all it is in expectation of such growth that votes are canvassed and debt legitimately incurred; for without growth in GNP there is no money to spare for paying off debts. No wonder politicians are tempted to put faith in the optimists. It is well documented that in a democracy those who are too far out in front of the people will not be returned to office. This is especially true if they promise today's consumer-driven electorate a Churchillian 'blood, toil, sweat and tears' when opposition parties are offering cheap energy and low taxes. We would all like to go to heaven, but nobody wants to die first.

However the solution lies not only in educating politicians. If we vote them out of office, they will re-educate themselves speedily enough. It is we, the people, who need to understand the issues. And then if the ship were indeed seen to be sinking, all hands would rush to man the pumps, as in a storm at sea. Two things have first to be done. One is to detach ourselves from purely monetary assessments of the future. These are simply misleading. The other is to look at how the economy operates in physical and biological terms; to bring some science to bear on the analysis of the economy because it is only through science that the environment can be incorporated.

The magnitude of the self-deception that can be wrought by thinking in monetary units is well illustrated by the comment of one well-known American economist (who will not be named lest some outraged environmental group sets out to lynch him), that global warming is of no concern to industrialised countries as very little of their GNP derives from climate-sensitive sectors of the economy like agriculture or forestry! This is like suggesting that because the liver is less than 1% of body weight its role is irrelevant to our health.

A Bonn idea

The 1997 Kyoto Protocol agreed that by 2010 all countries would have reduced their emissions to 1990 rates. This agreement had to be ratified by the governments, and in the majority of cases was not. A subsequent meeting in The Hague in 2000, also failed to reach agreement, mainly for two reasons. The USA refused to have anything to do with it, and the European Union took too hard a line for many delegations to accept, especially the Japanese.

The conference reconvened in July 2001 at Bonn. After a mammoth final session lasting forty-eight hours, an agreement was reached and announced at 10.20 am on the 23rd July. It was hailed as a break-through. In fact to get everyone on board the European Union had to relax its standards, and major concessions had to be made to some countries, notably Japan. Still it was, as one delegate put it, 'one small step for mankind'. The United States, the world's biggest greenhouse gas emitter, still opted out. The entire burden of reducing emissions was placed for the moment upon thirty-nine industrialised countries

This is the compromise hammered out:

• Countries that met their targets could sell their spare emission rights to others (see in Chapter 9 the alternative idea of Personal Energy Rights).

• There would be no penalties for countries that failed to achieve their target, but for every million tonnes of carbon dioxide over their target they would be expected to reduce emissions by 1.3 million in the subsequent years.

• Countries could treat their forests as carbon sinks. This would apply not merely to new forests but existing ones.

The issue of carbon sinks is a tricky one because they are inevitably temporary. No tree grows for ever. If it is not cut down it will eventually decay, releasing greenhouse gases. If it is cut down, and used for firewood, then it immediately releases its carbon as carbon dioxide. If it is used in construction or as furniture, it will also have a limited lifetime, though possibly a century or more, but nonetheless limited, and very likely be burned as firewood or dumped when it will also decay.

The best that can be said for the Bonn Accord is that it is a beginning, and quite an achievement to get 180 delegations to agree on a wording. Now it remains to be seen what governments will make of this agreement.

Marketing sustainable development

There is already enough popular concern about the environment that politicians cannot brush it aside. Yet, as already noted, it presents them with terrible risks. Their solution is, as always, to find some form of words that carries the right message but is sufficiently ambivalent to leave plenty room for manoeuvre, rather like prime minister Blair's call to the 1999 Labour Party conference for progress in place of conservatism (small 'c'). The words *sustainable development* are a marketing executive's dream. They soothe a concerned public while being vague enough to avoid serious inconvenience to governments, industry or commerce. They are a shibboleth which has become the mantra of our times with which to exorcise the ambivalence of driving ahead with economic growth while deploring its effects.

This expression *sustainable development* has been in circulation now for almost twenty years. The social effect has been remarkable. Barely a speech omits a reference to it, be it from a politician or a corporate leader. Surely it has to mean more than a palliative to a concerned minority. Unhappily the words have been trivialised and adapted to new meanings. The language is evolving, and at the same time being politicised Today *sustainable development* means whatever the user chooses. To the haulage company it may imply better roads and cheaper fuel; to the Green lobby fewer vehicles. It invokes a little bit of energy efficiency here, some pollution abatement there, waste recycling or a carbon tax. All these separate initiatives are of course valuable and welcome but they are like pressing a faulty brake on a steep incline. We still hurtle towards an increasingly unsustainable state albeit at a slower pace. But it gives time to tighten one's seat belt, and contemplate our impending fate.

Some uses of the phrase are outright misrepresentations; take *sustainable city* for example. It is extremely improbable that any city is or can be sustainable, for cities depend on the countryside for food, oilwells for fuel, and lakes or wells for water. When Leningrad was besieged by the Nazis in 1942 it had to be self-sufficient in food, fuel and water for over a year. But when one counts the thousands who died of cold and hunger or the furniture and floor boards burnt to provide heat, one can hardly say it was a sustainable city. Indeed nothing and no-one is individually sustainable. We live by, on and through one another. For all of us the inter-connections run into hundreds, if not thousands. Each one of us is inevitably an agent in the world's economic evolution and so a burden on the environment. If you doubt this, reflect for a while on what you do with your income, even if you live simply and give it away or invest it.

Durable development

So let us reconsider the term *sustainable development*, or *sustainability* as it is more commonly expressed. Sustainable means, well – something which can be maintained. So sustainable development is a form of development that can be maintained. There is nothing ambiguous about that. Taken literally it implies no limited time horizon like the next election. It stretches into the far distance as blurred as the dun uplands of Tibet seen from the Himalayas. In view of the fact that the word has been hi-jacked it is time to reinvigorate the concept and restore its original sense of purpose, and indeed urgency. The authors therefore offer a fresh term, *durable development*: a durable economy and environment. What we need and seek is *durability*.

Till now, in an economic context, *sustainable development* has been open to interpretation in two quite different ways: either that the existing *level* of development can be maintained or that the *pace* of development can be sustained. Even if it is accepted that both interpretations can include protection of the environment, the difference between them is highly significant.

The first represents a steady-state or equilibrium situation, much like treading water to keep afloat. It says, 'We have got this far, let's see if we can maintain our material standard of living, while continuing to rescue the environment'. This is approximately the position taken by the green parties. Note that a state of equilibrium need not imply stagnation, but can be one of simultaneous growth and decay.

The second interpretation implies continued economic growth. It is the one adopted by politicians and by business and commerce. Growth is normally expressed as year upon year fractional increase. However small that percentage be, the effect is exponential. Growth is acceleration. Now as any car driver knows one cannot accelerate for ever. Eventually the car reaches a speed where the road and air friction match the power input from the engine. At this point of maximum speed, the fuel use per unit distance travelled is the least efficient. It requires force to create acceleration, and the source of that force is energy. These principles are not limited to the car. Societies also use energy to drive their economies. Could there come a point in development where the economic engine demands more fuel than can be made available or is environmentally acceptable? Indeed, that time seems to be upon us already in terms of greenhouse gas emissions. We all know, too, what happens to a car when it runs out of fuel: it stops. Many of us, seeing the fuel indicator low, ease off on our speed, hoping to reach the next petrol station. This may be a physical analogy, but it is a rather apt one. If the world runs short of energy there are no cosmic breakdown systems to come to our aid.

The populace has been led by the politicians and economists to accept the second interpretation of sustainable development, that of acceleration, to which economic theory conceives of no end, for money is infinitely expandable. Does this not suggest some defect in the underlying economic theory?

Governments, dithering between caution and ambition, are faced with chilling forecasts from their economists of the disastrous effects of reduced GNP.[7] So they fudge the decisions. This explains why at the inter-governmental meeting in Kyoto in 1997, the industrialised countries limited their commitments and agreed simply to restore their carbon dioxide emissions to 1990 rates by 2010. Indeed Article 2 of the final protocol states that the measures taken should be slow enough to allow '*economic development to proceed in a sustainable manner*'. How's that for specious wording?

The hope is always that human ingenuity will come to our aid with some technological fix. It is axiomatic in economic theory that scarcity will always stimulate the technology to produce a substitute, like aluminium to replace copper. But what if there can be no substitute? This is the case with energy, whose pivotal role in the economy has never been taken up by economists. It is true that some economists have factored energy into their equations, but always in terms of price. Even maintaining the current level of world development requires a continual (sustained!) input of energy amounting to the stupendous equivalent of ten billion tonnes of oil annually, and this, mark you, of a non-renewable finite resource. So if we want to go on expanding is it not wise to work out a strategy before we find the cupboard is finally becoming bare?

Could this really happen, you may ask? The answer is that it certainly need not, but it could if we fail to take appropriate action soon enough. If we do there is no reason why the human race should not manage a seamless transition from the second (accelerating) interpretation of sustainable development to the (stable) first. It is a further purpose of this book to suggest how this might be achieved, and what difficulties lie in the way. One thing is certain. The society of the future cannot be like that of today. The information revolution will be just that: a revolution. But it can't create energy. A virtual economy cannot substitute for a real economy. This is the topic for the next chapter.

Notes

1   Genesis 9:2.

2   UN Framework Convention on Climate Change (see www.unfcee.de).

3   Biosphere is a nice omnibus word for the natural environment around, below and above us.

4   *GEO 2000*, edited by Robin Clarke and published by Earthscan on behalf of

UNEP, 1999. Contact UNEP, Box 30552, Nairobi, Kenya.

5   *Business Week*, January 15, 2001, p 60.

6   Gross Domestic Product (GDP) is the value of all goods and services marketed in a country over one specific year. Gross National Product (GNP) takes account also of imports and exports.

7   Climate change and its impacts: Stabilisation of CO_2 in the Atmosphere. See www.met-office.gov.uk/sec5/CR_div/CoP5).

2

... But by energy too

Or like the snow falls in the river
A moment white – then melts forever
ROBERT BURNS

We pointed out in Chapter 1 that though money is an abstraction and cannot itself create physical wealth, it is still the means by which we manage our affairs. When it comes to the actual creation of physical wealth, that is dependent entirely on the application of energy. If you remain sceptical of such a pivotal role for energy, try this real-life experiment. Resolve for one day to rely solely upon the sun for energy, while still attempting to carry out your daily routine. This means using no gas, coal, petrol or electricity. You will be struck by the extent to which your life-style requires a continual input of energy. You cannot cook. You cannot maintain a warm environment (or in a tropical country, a cool one). You cannot move your car except by pushing it. You cannot use a bus or train. You cannot listen to the radio (unless you have clockwork radio) or watch TV. If it is dark you cannot see. And you cannot even use your word processor to record your thoughts or play your tapes and CDs to ease the troubled spirit!

Suppose that you have entered into this experiment with gusto, and have armed yourself with a tin-opener, canned food, a good book, a pen, a notepad, a bicycle and a magnifying glass (to concentrate the sun's rays). You may get through one day happily enough. But bear in mind that all those things you have brought with you, not to mention the shoe leather and bicycle tyres you have worn down, have all been produced somewhere else by someone else, and that the people who produced them used energy not only to support their own life-styles, but to run the machines that produced the goods, the books and the food and deliver them to the shops. In other words neither you, nor anyone else, can live an energy-free life-style. We are all hooked on energy to some degree or other!

Energy can relieve many burdens, and offer wider horizons. Fed to a tractor, it relieves the back-breaking toil of ploughing with horses or oxen. A can of diesel can replace a lot of drudgery. Spanish trawlers can make quick forays 1500 miles into Hebridean waters and Japanese trawlers can drag nets fifteen miles long in the Indian Ocean in their quest for tuna. Half a tonne of jet fuel will be your share of the energy that flies you to your long-haul holiday destination. Energy plays such an important role in all production processes that firms struggling to stay afloat in the competitive globalised economy demand that it be cheap. The conventional wisdom has been to open up energy markets to competition. As a result, dozens of companies now besiege consumers with offers of cheaper gas and electricity. The effect is to increase consumption, which is good for individual company profits, but it also means we are running through our inheritance of energy resources even faster. Not only that, the end products of energy use are the world's greatest source of pollution. Cheap energy inevitably encourages waste and unnecessary emissions. There has to be a better solution, and there is. We return to it later. But like an unravelled ball of string, the energy equation is not easily disentangled.

Yet are we perhaps crying wolf? There is still plenty of oil, coal, natural gas, oil shales and uranium[1] lying in the earth. According to the British Petroleum company's 1999 *Review of World Energy* there are, at current rates of global consumption, some 35 years of proven oil reserves. Optimists believe even more oil will be discovered. Moreover the sun beams down energy upon us at a rate ten thousand times greater than the world's current rate of energy consumption. Surely in due course, if and when all the Earth's energy stores have been used up, it is just a matter of capturing those rays? As will be seen in Chapter 5, that would indeed be possible, but would not be all that easy. There is a lot of mis-information floating around. Some, like Greenpeace, advocate an immediate switch to renewable energies, arguing that further exploration for oil is unnecessary and nuclear reactors could soon be shut down. Alas, this is but a forlorn hope. A dynamic analysis of the investment requirements for renewables demonstrates that it would take considerable time, maybe a century, to achieve a renewable-based economy, and that were we to follow Greenpeace's advocacy we would have to accept extreme energy penury[2] and a much lower material standard of living for many years. Society is not at all ready for that. Given a choice between caution (incurring discomfort) and risk, it chooses risk. Look at the mortality on the roads; thirty-five thousand people killed on the UK's roads in ten years which is many times the mortality from the world's worst nuclear disaster at Chernobyl. Most drivers break the speed limits. And although road deaths are deplored by all, there is still no lobby to banish cars, even by Greenpeace. The fact is that most of us find it easy enough to live with Faustian bargains like fast cars and nuclear energy when the alternative is cold, misery and draughty bus stops. But we need to have a clear idea of the extent of those bargains.

It is certainly true that technology can be engaged to advance our material welfare as well as offering remarkable opportunities to diminish our consumption of resources and deal with unwanted pollution. The danger is to imagine that we can at the same time continue to go on living as before – wasteful and careless. Politicians agonising over their responsibilities behave like some learner driver with one foot on the accelerator while the other fidgets with the brake. Once again the prospects are obscured by the recourse to purely financial methods of analysis, using dubious cost-benefit analysis techniques and the primacy of the profit motive.

It is here that science, with its capacity to measure using nature's laws, has a contribution to make. Science can inform us how, and at what rate, we may substitute for the dwindling stocks of fossil energy to support the level of economic growth politicians are counting on or to make the transition to a sustainably-fuelled world. It can inform us which economic goals are physically possible and, for those that are not, what changes in policy need to be introduced to meet given objectives. It can inform us what choices have to be made concerning our lifestyles if we finally decide to make true sustainability (durability) the goal of our society. Of special significance, since we are dealing with the long term, is the fact that science makes measurements in terms which remain constant whether we are looking ten, fifty or a hundred years ahead. By contrast (as we have already remarked) money, the unit of measurement of the economist, changes unpredictably over time, and increasingly so as the time horizon lengthens.[3] Imagine the impossibility of designing a bridge if the unit of length arbitrarily changed each day!

You may well at this point be asking yourself a few questions. Why, if science really has something important to contribute to economics, do we not meet scientists in university economics departments or government treasuries? Why are the physical implications of economic growth not taken into account as a matter of course?

What has been lacking is a physical method of quantifying the economy to parallel the monetary approach. This has now been done, as will be explained in greater detail in Chapter 6, but the fact that an alternative possibility exists has yet to percolate deep into economic territory.[4] The sticking point here is the lack of co-ordination between two very different paradigms; in other words two very different ways of looking at things. Science adopts nature's laws, which are rigorous and timeless. Economics has no laws in the strict sense of the word, only empirical rules and precepts which are used to interpret and enumerate human behaviour through the medium of price. It is rigorous enough, though, compared to the financial system which is close to being out of control.

Part of the problem is the compartmentalisation of knowledge. Over the centuries the human race has accrued a vast reservoir of knowledge. Huge intellectual advances have been achieved through specialisation. But this has its dangers. Experts in one discipline no longer talk the same language as those in others. In particular the two cultures of science and economics have barely any meeting point. The economics profession has traditionally been given free rein to look after the economy with the result that we behave as if there were no tomorrow. The scientists have tacitly yielded, devoting their own talents to finding out what makes things tick. Engineers have applied that knowledge to the practical domain of technology. Business then turns this into profit. And why not? But the partition of knowledge, the separation of action from consequences, is the very antithesis of the holistic approach needed for the analysis of what really constitutes development that is durable.

How different it was two centuries ago. In the Edinburgh of that time Adam Smith, the economist, David Hume, the philosopher and James Hutton, the founding father of geology, met in the street, dined and argued together. They were also farmers, scientists, inventors and administrators. Euler and Bernoulli interacted in Basle. Voltaire, the author, de Bougainville, the explorer, Fourier, the mathematician, and Lavoisier, the chemist, all lived in a Paris that was then a compact city. They could share each other's knowledge and wisdom. Today not one of us can absorb the huge body of skills and understanding that has been built up in these last two centuries. However, what we can do, indeed must do, is to link up the relevant parts of economics and science within a single system which includes both nature and the economy.

Let us start with nature's paradigm. Lift a pebble from off the beach, any pebble, and look at it. It is unique. No other is exactly identical. It has its own shape, colour, texture and weight. At the same time it shares an identical chemical structure with many others. Geologists are not concerned with the individual identity of this little stone, one of millions, even billions on that same sea shore. They are interested in how it came to be there and from whence it originated. They have studied the Earth and found sills, beds, intrusions, moraines and fossils. Their theories of evolution are based upon extensive observation and measurement. James Hutton gave civilisation its first holistic picture of the Earth's structure in his *Theory of the Earth,* published in 1788 and postulating that past events could be explained in terms of the processes of erosion and renewal that remain at work today. We have come to accept ideas like these, even some of the more mind-bending, such as that whole continents, once joined, are drifting apart in one place and bumping together at another. America and Europe are approaching each other at the rate of 5 centimetres a year.

The essence of science is that it seeks an underlying pattern within which facts make sense. Indeed amongst scientists this research aim is pursued with all the conviction of King Arthur's knights seeking the holy grail. Their zeal has paid off, and science today sits within a structure of physical laws that are seemingly incontrovertible, offering us amazing insights into how the physical world works. The much sought after 'grand unified theory', the scientists' equivalent of the free market philosophy that would link the strong nuclear forces with the theory of electromagnetic forces, is still beyond the grasp of physicists. Few doubt, however, that the physical laws of nature are immutable and represent a framework within which we can explain the provenance and chemistry of the individual stone on the beach, and move on from there to explain why planes fly, how to compute a geo-stationary orbit for a satellite or how to alter the genetic structure of an animal or plant cell. These are remarkable achievements, and they are possible because the fledgling scientist is trained to see his or her new knowledge lying within an established intellectual structure.

Economics, too, has its own intellectual structure, but the task is greater because it deals with people, whose actions are never entirely predictable. Imagine we are looking down at a crowd on the move, say from the lofty vantage of the apex of the duomo in Florence or the top gallery of the Eiffel Tower. Far below little human figures are scurrying about, no doubt with inner purpose, but to the casual observer seemingly at random. Economic theory, however, would have us believe that each one is a self-optimising, rational individual bent upon maximising her or his personal material welfare; a unique two-footed species known as h*omo economicus*. This hypothesis is central to the economist's intellectual view of the economy.[5] Of course, they know and we know that it is a gross simplification. Altruism is not dead. We each of us carry in our minds some historical experience that makes us cautious of our greed. Even the economist Nobel prize-winner Paul Samuelson once admitted, 'Man does not live by GNP alone'.

The dice are loaded against the economist in a search for an ultimate theorem, for unlike the stones on the beach as subjects of analysis, human beings have free will. Examples of *homo economicus* do indeed exist, but may not be a sufficiently representative sample of the human race to be a reliable basis for forecasting. Economics is necessarily a behavioral science, dealing with the uncertainty of human perception and the fickleness of consumer loyalty. Still, although there are no perfect markets and consumers do not have perfect information, economists have nevertheless visualised a structure within which their model of the human psyche can fit. Here the intersection of supply with demand is through price and income, where the prices set by all suppliers meet the income available to all purchasers. This is called an *equilibrium* model, even though logically a system at equilibrium cannot grow.

The usefulness of these models is questionable writes William Sherden, the author of *The Fortune Sellers*.[6] In his analysis of the forecaster's art he suggests that if you want to know where the economy is headed, don't ask an economist. He examined twelve studies that analysed forecasts between 1970 and 1995, and concluded: 'Economic forecasters have routinely failed to foresee turning points in the economy: the coming of severe recessions, the start of recoveries, the periods of increases or decreases of inflation'. Quoting the analysis of Professor Victor Zarnowitz of the University of Chicago, he records that of six top economic forecasting groups (including the US Federal Reserve Board) 46 out of 48 predictions missed the turning points.

Sherden, perhaps with his tongue in his cheek, has enunciated the first law of economics: 'that for every economist there is an equal and opposing economist',[7] and the second law that 'they are both wrong'. His analysis of economic forecasting makes interesting reading, but one suspects that he takes too little account of feedback effects.

The distinction between economics and science is as great as between the use of zero to indicate nothing, and its attachment to a number to indicate a factor of ten; but each has its place. The important point is that economics can tell us where people would *like* to go, and science where they *can* go. An action can only be economically feasible if in fact it is physically possible. Vision is not enough, for vision can speed ahead of reality.

We humans do not respond well to reality. We prefer beliefs and hope. If someone tells us 'the sky will be thick with the wings of chickens coming home to roost' we will treat this as a metaphor, implying there is trouble ahead. But for whom? Not us, surely. If in our anxiety we ask experts to check on the outlook they may employ tools called economic models. But these are metaphors too, and since they are couched in mathematical terms and are the fruit of much research, we tend to believe them. The trouble with such models is that they concentrate on but one aspect of the future: our potential well-being, ignoring anything whose monetary value cannot be measured..

If policies are to be formulated that can lead towards durable development, we need a model which can encapsulate the physical factors that underlie the economy and environment, including land, resources, environment and energy. Only then are we in a position to assess the potential of the system of which we are a part.

A simple example of a physical model would be one which forecast the optimum angle of the trajectory of a stone shot from an elastic catapult in order to achieve maximum distance; something many children do by intuition. It is 30 degrees from the horizontal. A more sophisticated model will take into account side wind, air resistance and the density of stone. Economies, though, are too complex to be reduced to a problem as simple as this.

The essential contribution of any model of the economy is to project into the future, to plot the dynamics of the changing system. Models using economic methods (anticipating human behaviour) do well enough for two or three years. Thereafter they become increasingly unreliable as people's preferences change, or new technologies enter the scene. If certain critical factors are omitted because the model builders didn't see them as important at the time, then the model and its outcome will be even less useful. One of the commonest omissions is energy because the conventional economic model of production expresses output as a function only of labour and capital (see footnote 8 in Chapter 1 or the appendix to Chapter 5). It seems that in economics there is no paradigm by which the price of energy can be forecast.

Scientific, physically-based models do not and cannot reflect human behaviour in the way economic models do. However, what they can do is to determine the limiting factors in the evolution of an economic system. In other words, apply a measure of reality to financial fantasy.[8]

There need not be any conflict of interest between economics and the application of science to economic evaluation. Both have their uses. Determining the economy's potential, that is identifying the available options in physical terms, is akin to calculating how much fuel is needed to fire a satellite into space. The objective is pre-stated: so much weight into such and such an orbit. If calculations show that this weight or that fuel charge cannot achieve the objective, then either the objective or the means must be re-considered. The proper task of economics is much like that of the person whose responsibility it is, equipped with those facts, to plan the logistics of the space project and carry it through to its final outcome. Take the sort of issues now facing humankind: enhancing global material prosperity, ending hunger and other deprivations, working towards a sustainable environment, and finding jobs for all. These are targets everyone will agree are worthwhile. The question is whether all can be achieved without having to give up anything – at least for a time. The politicians and economists between them may hammer out targets. It needs a physical assessment to see if they are mutually attainable. If they are not, then it is back to the drawing board for a re-design.

Every individual has a dream of the future. Some of it may be market-driven: the desire implanted for technological toys such as faster and more comfortable cars. Some of it may be driven by the need to escape the poverty of the past, and some of it may be no more than a pathetic struggle to acquire food and decent drinking water. There is no argument but that continued world development is needed. But development is not the same as acceleration. Sound, sensible development can mean change, even deceleration. The trouble with money as a unit of measure is that the mind takes liberties when it is unconstrained by physical reality. It is not enough to leave the future to the politicians or the economists. Neil Gunn, a novelist, put it this way in his foreword to *The Green Isle of the Great Deep*:

'The revolving earth, pitted with its tragedies, cried in a far voice from the middle of space; you cannot leave me to the politicians.

But the politicians, administrators, are needful, are necessary. To fulfil their high function they work with the cunning of the head. But to leave destiny to the head is to leave the trigger to the finger. And after the trigger is pulled, they cry above the desolation – (and the desolation was terrible to behold). ...

It cannot be left to them; not solely to them. You have to bring in wise men.'

As the twenty-first millennium opens with an almost universal acceptance that market forces are the correct basis for decision-making, we need to deal with the illusion that those forces are truly self-regulating. This is the stuff of the next chapter.

Notes

1   There is a paradox here between ample supplies and impending scarcity. In 1995 the group managing director of Shell Oil, John Jennings, stated that there were 1800 billion barrels of oil in proven reserves, with world consumption running at 65 billion barrels per year, so that at current rates of use there were only 28 years supply in hand. Four years later the BP figures suggested 35 years in hand.

2   In 1993 the Stockholm Environmental Institute published a report suggesting that by 2100, renewables could provide 2.5 times the world's energy demand. This claim is not without foundation, but the problem lies in what happens between now and then, and how we will find the means to invest in the systems needed.

3   The famous nineteenth-century physicist, Lord Kelvin, once remarked, 'When you can measure what you are speaking about, and express it in numbers, you know something about it: when you cannot express it in numbers, your knowledge is of a meagre and unsatisfactory kind. It may be the beginning of knowledge, but you have scarcely, in your thoughts,

advanced to the stage of science'. Paul Samuelson, an equally famous econ-omist quoted this in his oft re-issued textbook on economics, unaware, one supposes, of the irony in so doing.

4   Models of the economy using this approach are called natural capital accounting models, and have now been developed for Europe, the UK, the Netherlands and Australia.

5   Economics students are themselves rejecting these tired conventions. Twenty-seven Cambridge post-graduate economics students have published their critique in an e-mail newsletter called *Post-autistic Economics* (as at 18/10/01). See www.paecon.net

6   *The Fortune Sellers*, William A.Sherden, 1998, John Wiley, New York.

7   As in mechanics: for every force there exists and equal and opposite force.

8   This was very well brought out in the 1999 film *Rogue Trader*, depicting the rise and fall of the young derivatives trader Nick Leeson, who worked for Barings Bank in Singapore. He ruined the bank.

3

One thing leads to another

Every why has a wherefore.
SHAKESPEARE, *THE COMEDY OF ERRORS*

Market forces alone, mediated through money, cannot lead to a durable future. They represent but a limited part of the world in which we live. To act wisely we need to understand the feedbacks and signals operating within the wider system and between the different sub-systems. Only then does it become possible to control the forces of globalisation and to reconcile human demands with the realities of the biosphere.

Systems may look complex, but are really nothing more than a mass of interacting relationships each one of which may be quite straightforward. In the first place, nothing happens without a cause. If your friend is struck by lightning you may take the view that it was the wrath of God. But there is a simple physical explanation for the lightning, and a rather more complex one for the place it happens to strike. When we, as individuals, initiate an action, we do so in the expectation that our action is the cause of what follows. The outcome is an event. We are accustomed by our experience of life to accept that there is a relation between cause and effect.

Less familiar is the idea that an effect can, directly or indirectly, then influence the cause. When this happens it is called feedback. Often that link is so tenuous as to be unrecognised. Cause-effect-cause, though, is an endless loop that inhabits virtually every aspect of our lives from the homeostasis, or self-regulation, that controls our body temperature to the workings of the market economy. It governs the seasons and the climate, the motion of waves and much else besides. And in human affairs, buffeted as we are by immense global economic forces, the feedbacks need to be identified if we are to secure some measure of control over our future. The system of which each one of us is a part is essentially deterministic but, like the weather, unpredictable. The ship of state may have a rudder, but if no-one is at the helm reacting intelligently to the waves, then chance not wisdom takes over.

When a cause stimulates an event, change occurs. Things are now different from the previous state of affairs. The difference, when detected, is called a signal. A signal is the bearer of information. All control consists of identifying a signal, then using the information to modify the system's performance. If you are tired or in pain, this is a signal from your body to your mind. Cutting off the signal with a painkiller or a stimulant doesn't put anything right, and may even exacerbate the ailment within. To observe a signal and then disregard it is foolish. One ignores the oil warning light on the car's dashboard at one's peril. One can choose to be fatalistic, but most people will seek to either replenish the oil or find the problem.

Feedback can trigger growth, decay or stability. An example of growth would be an interest-bearing savings account. The amount in the account coupled to the rate of interest represents the cause. The effect is the monetary interest thereby generated. One can intervene and withdraw the interest as an income, or let it accumulate in which case it feeds back in a positive way and amplifies the deposit and so, as time passes, affects the cause. The more you have the more you get; an agreeable experience. At 10% interest, the sum doubles every seven years. This is known as positive feedback and results in exponential growth. Bankers, with unconscious irony, call such a feedback loop a virtuous circle.

Unchecked positive feedback, as in cancer, always contains within it the seeds of disaster sometime in the future. But in all systems sooner or later it is countered by what is called negative feedback. An example is the body's reaction to de-hydration. Thirst is a signal which prompts us to drink and which, if ignored, will eventually result in death. Hunger is another example. At the heart of all stable systems there are one or more negative feedback loops at work.

Though it may be far from obvious, close inspection of any system of organisation will reveal it to contain at least one positive and one negative feedback loop. This is why no system ever expands for ever. Some negative feedback, perhaps deeply hidden, comes along to stop growth. A simple, homely example is fermenting grapes to make wine. If you're into home brewing you will know that things go slowly to begin with, then speed up, but that after a while fermentation ceases. What is happening is that each yeast cell splits into two. Two become four, four become eight and so on. The more there are the more they become; positive feedback. This is reflected in the ever steepening slope of the yeast population plot in Figure 3.1. The cells convert sugar in the grapes into alcohol. Eventually, however, one of two things happens: either the yeast cells run out of sugar and starvation sets in or the alcohol content rises to the point where it effectively pollutes and poisons them.

Here, then, is a system of one positive feedback and two negative feedbacks.

In a low sugar grape, fermentation ceases through lack of sugar and yields say, sauvignon blanc, while with a high-sugar grape the cells die from alcohol poisoning and the result is, say, sauternes.

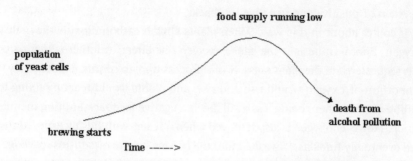

Figure 3.1: The change in growth rate of yeast cells during fermentation.

It takes little imagination to see this example of grape fermentation as an allegory of the human condition. Were we to run out of energy (sugar) our civilisation would be bound to perish. If we overdo the growth thing, we may die of pollution. The trick may well be to find the highest point of the curve and, having made the best of our situation, stay there. The human race has multiplied through the feedback loop of births exceeding deaths. Like the yeast cells, the human population should have crashed long ago through lack of food, as Malthus predicted. But we learned to intensify our agriculture and economy through the application of fossil energy. This has allowed us to extend the rising part of the curve in Figure 3.1. Everyone knows that part of the price has been massive and increasing environmental pollution. If we run short of energy we will soon be over the peak and slipping down the far side! And we won't be drinking sauternes either. Many past civilisations grew, declined and finally perished as they overstretched their resource base or became over-populated.

With our ability now to analyse and understand the system it should not be beyond our powers to create a durable economy and environment by legislating for appropriate negative feedback loops, like the checks and balances of a democratic legal system.

The Gaia hypothesis

This concept, first enunciated by the biologist James Lovelock, views the natural world as a dynamic system of interacting positive and negative feedbacks; a sort of global homeostasis parallel to that which maintains our own bodies in chemical balance and within a narrow temperature range. The Gaia hypothesis explains how it comes about that the fraction of oxygen in the atmosphere remains close to 21%, and has been so for about three hundred million years. And a good thing too, because if it rose to 25% natural vegetation would catch fire, and if it fell to 17% animals and humans could not survive. That 21% zone is critical to our survival, and it remains at this level because the atmosphere is governed by a system of positive and negative feedbacks.

It comes about in this way. When plants absorb carbon dioxide they release oxygen. Photosynthesis is the cause; oxygen one effect. Another is that carbon gets sequestered in the plant mass. If this process were to continue indefinitely the proportion of oxygen would rise and rise, and plants would react by fixing less carbon dioxide, there being less available: a negative feedback limiting the interaction. However oxygen is also removed when it reacts with freshly exposed rocks and eventually finds itself washed into the oceans, where organisms scavenge it. These eventually die and, in the absence of air, anaerobically decompose to release methane which, once it reaches the atmosphere, reacts with oxygen to produce carbon dioxide. Thus the earth's habitable atmosphere is maintained by a complex chain of positive and negative feedbacks. The periodicity of this cycle is of the order of thousands of years.

Lovelock's ideas have not been universally accepted. He himself commented: 'When I first introduced Gaia, I had vague hopes that it might be denounced from the pulpit and thus made acceptable to my scientific colleagues. As it was, Gaia was embraced by theologians, and by a wide range of New Age writers and thinkers, but denounced by the biologists'.[1]

More recently computer models have been built which support the Gaia hypothesis, even to predicting the present oxygen ratio in the atmosphere.

Criteria

If we, as a society, wish to control and shape our future we need to go one step further than simply understanding the feedbacks at work. We need to set up criteria by which to judge the signals, and then take action. That action might well turn out to be a new law or regulation.

Take the simple example of a domestic central heating system. In this case the criterion of success, the desired room temperature, is ours to choose, but set by the capacity of the furnace, or boiler. The signal that fires the boiler is the difference between the desired (selected) temperature and the actual temperature of the room. When the desired and actual temperature are the same the signal becomes zero, and the boiler shuts down. The signal and the resulting action oppose each other, so it is negative feedback. Now imagine what would happen if a careless electrician had reversed the wires so that when the room temperature exceeded the desired value, the signal triggered the boiler to fire up more fiercely. This would be positive feedback. The difference between the signal and the criterion would get bigger and bigger, and the room hotter and hotter. Unrestrained positive feedback always ends in disaster of one sort or another. An atom bomb is one example. Lemming populations are another. They breed rapidly. The more lemmings, the more lemmings; an exponential growth in lemmings. When they outstrip the food available, the population crashes, and it is left to the few survivors to bring forward the next wave of lemmings. This is very typical of an unstable or uncontrolled system which oscillates between peaks and troughs, like the swings between a bear and a bull market. The rising part of the well-known Kondratiev business cycle[2] can be explained as a case of monetary output beginning to outpace physical backing. This leads to unsupportable debt, and the economy falls back till it is again in phase with physical reality.

Just as we desire a certain level of warmth, we would presumably prefer to live in a stable economic and environmental system, rather than one that goes from boom to bust; from dizzy growth to recession; from global warming to ice age. If so, a set of appropriate negative feedbacks needs to be put in place. We cannot alter the physics of the natural world, but we can and should control the economic forces that so deeply affect our lives so that they are in congruence with what nature can provide.

Interpreting signals

'One swallow does not make a summer', said Aristotle. Making an interpretation from just one piece of information can be risky. The rising barometer does not always herald better weather. A red sky at night may be the shepherd's delight, but a riotous sunset can be succeeded by a drizzly morning. The system may be more complex than we imagine. So having noted the signal as being different from the criterion, what should be done about it? To take an example of current concern to society: if unemployment exceeds an acceptable level of around three per cent, what action should we take? Stimulate economic growth, which is the conventional wisdom, reduce wages, shorten the working week, or encourage cost-free leisure pursuits? Whatever action is taken will not only affect the unemployment level, but also many other aspects of the economy: reduced wages may result in poverty; free leisure pursuits may require higher taxes to support them. It is an observable fact that in these over-regulated and politically correct times, many a well-intended piece of legislation interferes with the logical working of earlier, more fundamental legislation. We should therefore seek out and understand all the other relevant feedbacks in the system. In short a holistic analysis is needed in order to make rational decisions.

These days it is very popular to create indicators of environmental quality:

levels of particulate matter in the atmosphere, for example, rate of species loss or rates of depletion of physical resources. Again, if measurement shows they are falling below ideal norms, what steps are to be taken? Less economic growth? More investment in pollution control? Exporting polluting industries? If these measures conflict with other criteria, say unemployment to take our previous example, then conflict arises. This is why a real search for durable development must be made in a quantitative way bringing together both physical and economic factors.

A first step towards an understanding is always to trace the links between causes and effects. Anyone can do this, and it can be a highly self-educating procedure. The reader should try it out for the case of the grape fermentation discussed earlier and whose results were depicted in Figure 3.1. Simply ask yourself what is the effect when any one cause becomes larger. Start by writing down the name of any element in the system, say yeast population, but it could equally well be alcohol strength or sugar stock. Then ask yourself the question, 'If the yeast population increases what other things in the system are affected; which would increase, which decrease?' Well, yeast population affects the rate of fermentation. Write down 'rate of fermentation', and draw an arrow from the former to the latter. If in your view more yeast means faster fermentation, then place a plus sign at the head of the arrow to indicate a positive relationship.

Now consider what is affected by the rate of fermentation. It increases the rate at which alcohol is produced. What is the source of the alcohol? Obviously the sugar in the grapes. So draw an arrow from sugar to alcohol, also with a positive sign at its head. This process reduces the stock of sugar so an arrow should go from alcohol back to sugar, the sign at the arrow head is negative (minus). So far we have not identified any loops, but they are there.

Two of the effects have been more alcohol and less sugar, so ask yourself again what effect is there when either one of these increases. In the case of sugar it affects the amount of fermentation, so that an arrow from sugar to rate of fermentation will have a positive sign on the arrowhead. In the case of alcohol, it will reduce the rate of fermentation. Then finally we need a link between rate of fermentation and yeast population. This will be a positive relationship.

Now the rule to find out whether a loop is positive or negative is that you multiply all the signs in the loop. Under the rules of arithmetic a plus (+) times a minus (-) is a minus, while a plus times a plus is positive and a minus times a minus is also positive. Enter the product of the signs in the space between the loops. You will find one positive and two negative loops.

Yeast population ——> rate of cell division ——> yeast population (positive)

Rate of fermentation ——> sugar stock ——> rate of fermentation (negative)

Rate of fermentation ———> alcolohol produced ———> rate of fermentation (negative)

Figure 3.2 summarises the picture. It is called an influence diagram, and is a very handy way of clarifying one's thoughts. The signs in brackets indicate the nature of the feedback loop.

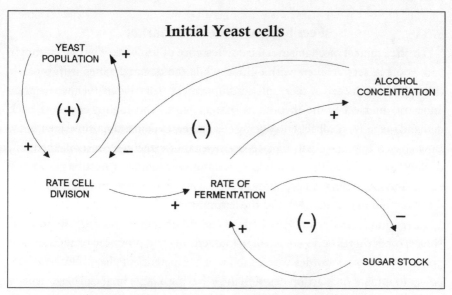

Figure 3.2 An influence diagram of the fermentation of sugar to alcohol

Delayed information

Most information is out of date by the time you get it. This is especially true of environmental and economic information where it may take a year or more to assemble the data that can deliver a signal. Delay affects the quality of decision making. A good driver senses a corner, and steers smoothly round it. A drunk driver is slow to interpret events. Such delay can be fatal. For governments, the difficulties involved in anticipating the effects of existing policies and conditions pose enormous problems when seeking to exercise some understanding and control of the economy and environment.

A prevailing approach is to engage experts to make a money-based computer model of the economy which, supplied with last year's data and previous trends, will hopefully forecast the future. However, buried in these models are the historical habits of consumers expressed in monetary units. The consumer is notoriously fickle so that a reliable projection of two years is about the best one can hope for. The differences in approach, as in their conclusions, between one economic modeller and another are enormous, and quite discouraging to decision makers not versed in modelling, that is to say most people. And which modeller is to be believed? By contrast a model based on physical laws is much less open to dispute. For example a relatively simple physical model of the Earth's natural processes can replicate hundreds of thousands of years of evolution. A bio-physical model of the economy can replicate considerably more than a decade.

Feedback and the free market

The free market mechanism is the quintessence of feedback. The cost of supply of a good or service alters with output, while the demand varies with price. If through research each of these relationships can be determined, then where price and cost intersect is the theoretical market price. Too high a cost cuts back demand (negative feedback). Reducing cost increases demand (positive feedback). Low cost in one place will replace higher cost elsewhere. Prices will therefore decline[3] as the most efficient producers capture the market. Consumers will buy more, thus expanding the economy *ad infinitum*. Does that sound familiar? Does it not remind one of the plight of the lemmings?

In economic analysis efficiency is perceived as output per unit labour cost. Hence, other things being equal, all manufacturing and provision of services will gravitate to those countries where labour is competent but cheap. But since the power to initiate such action lies with those having a large financial base, usually multinational companies, many workers in the once affluent western democracies will eventually be pauperised, and with them their capacity to buy goods. On the other hand it will take a long time for the low wage earners in the developing world to replace the enormous buying power of consumers in the western developed countries; but it could happen. This is a negative feedback yet to be entered into contemporary economic models. The solution, according to the prime minister of Malaysia, Mahathir Mohamed, is to couple free movement of capital with free movement of people. Now, that's real globalisation. It would put the fear of death into the industrialised countries!

This trend towards poverty within a workforce will be exacerbated by the emergence of a form of e-commerce used by large companies to drive down the prices of their source materials. The idea is as follows. Say a number of companies need strip steel for their factories, the sort of thing used to make cars, washing machines, etc. They collectively post their needs on the internet, and invite suppliers to quote. This is then an auction on a global scale, and the forces of competition will drive down prices. The manufacturing companies will now be able to make bigger profits or lower their prices. When we built a computer model to study this effect on a global scale we were astonished at what we found. Two things happened. First wages, and therefore purchasing power, were driven down. As a result overall demand fell, even though products were cheaper. Profits for shareholders rose considerably at first, but were then eroded as demand fell. A further consequence was that workers' income fell in relation to shareholder income; this did the shareholders little good, because with falling demand, their absolute income then fell in the long run. A prosperous society is one where gains are shared.

The free market operates on ruthless feedback. It does not work in the long-term interests of the human population at large, but only of those who own the capital. Just recently, according to the late Dana Meadows,[4] the 84 richest people in the world control assets worth more than the total income of China's 1.2 billion people. The wealth of just 225 billionaires is equal to the annual incomes of just under half of the global population.

At the same time there is some sand in the works. The first and most obvious defect is that there is no such thing as a totally free market, and rightly so. A totally free market would be anarchy, pure positive feedback. All governments intervene to some degree to safeguard certain classes of people or trade or environment; many of us think insufficiently so in many cases. Still, the most favoured groups are the large corporations and financial services. The second drawback is that the free market theory depends on an assumption that there is good information on the prices of all alternative goods and services; that all people have access to this information and these alternatives. This is certainly not the case, though we are constantly told that with internet commerce on the increase it soon will be. One wonders. The third flaw is the most important of all. A market that works through prices can only be successful if money is not being artificially created at a greater rate than true wealth. As we shall see in the next chapter, this is not the case either.

In a system that quantifies everything in terms of price there can be no such thing as absolute scarcity, of there being nothing left. Both theory and observation inform us that scarcity induces prices to rise, which will stimulate the emergence of a substitute. This is negative feedback. Aluminium can and does replace copper as an electrical conductor, plastics can and do replace metal parts. But this way of thinking can also be a delusion. Some years ago one of the authors was at a chemical engineering convention in New York where he listened to the keynote address of the pulp and paper group. It was explained that inevitably forest sources of pulp would one day be constrained, and the time was not far off when 'paper' would be made from petroleum-based plastic. Next day he heard the keynote speaker in the petroleum group, who prophesied that as oil and gas resources diminished the world would be turning more and more to substitutes based on forest products. Now both forecasts cannot be true.

The theory breaks down completely where there is *no* substitute. This is the case with energy. There is no substitute for energy. The fact that energy is the driving force of the economy makes it a rather special case. That is why this book will devote a fair bit of space to its role and availability.

It is often said these days that globalisation has gone so far that governments cannot really take much corrective action in defence of their citizens. This has come about because they have deliberately given away their power, rather than having had it taken from them. Everybody should read David Korten's excellent analysis of corporate capitalism in his *When Corporations Rule the World.*[5] His analysis is a first step towards a solution. The next is to find and legislate for those feedbacks that will disempower the global corporations. Globalisation cannot in any case continue unfettered for that would ultimately lead to revolution. Hopefully intelligent action will make it unnecessary.

Stability and equilibrium

At the moment the world economic system in GNP terms is on the rising curve of the left-hand part of Figure 3.1 The peak is still to come.[6] It is quite possible, though, that with wise government the growth curve can reach equilibrium, avoiding overall decline, but rising and falling here and there.

A durable system will be stable, but not necessarily unchanging. As anyone who has visited the Uffizi in Florence will know, such is the press of visitors that there is always a queue. Only as one tourist emerges is another let in. The composition of the spectators is constantly changing, the equilibrium population inside the gallery is stable. At a cocktail party the noise level rises and rises as guests arrive. One has to speak ever louder to be able to communicate. This is positive feedback. But at a certain intensity the noise level peaks, for by now the negative feedbacks have become as strong as the positive. These are the effects of incomprehension which result in inane, but silent nodding or shaking of heads or of sheer weariness on the part of those with poor hearing. In some cases guests abandon conversation in favour of drink. The peak noise level is an equilibrium set by many contributors each acting in different ways. Experience tells us that if we remove the external input – drink – the noise level quickly declines.

Thus stability embraces simultaneous growth and decline. Because money does not differentiate between one type of goods and another, to an economist a stable system could be one where manufacturing declines, but service activities expand to create the same income. As will be clear in later chapters a certain amount of manufacturing is essential to underpin the economy. To a conservationist a stable system may be one where the environment remains intact, whatever is happening to the economy. A durable system will be one where both economic and environmental objectives are met, and the energy supply is assured.

However even inherently stable systems can oscillate dangerously if the time-lag between the signal and subsequent action is greater than the response time. It is then difficult to know what is the right policy. Picture a yacht rolling in a heavy sea. The roll can be dampened by good design and intelligent seamanship, but if the sea becomes too stormy the negative feedback signal may be too slow in relation to other events such as a huge maverick wave, and the boat may turn turtle. However a well-designed yacht will always pop up again, albeit with a very wet crew. In economic and environmental situations, where there are considerable time lags between an effect and its being observed, the system may oscillate wildly from one extreme to the next. It is not impossible that certain of our actions (collectively) could generate one oscillation too far in the natural world and result in irrevocable damage; damage, that is, to us for nature would ultimately reassert herself. This is the inherent worry about global warming and the current debate over the significance of the human contribution to atmospheric carbon dioxide.

A system out of control is one with exponential, or ever increasing, growth where positive feedback always exceeds negative feedback. Such is the monetary system. Here complexity is amplified by human perception or, one should say, mis-perception. It only took a minor upward movement in the value of the Japanese currency vis-à-vis the dollar, in October 1998, for a catastrophic change to take place in the value of certain hedge funds.

Natural systems, as the Gaia hypothesis explains, tend towards overall stability, though nature herself is far from quiescent. Witness the recent tropical storms in Asia and the Caribbean which are said to have destroyed the accumulated infrastructure of twenty to forty years of human effort and investment. Nature has so often put a spoke in our wheels in the form of cataclysms, disease, ice ages and global warming. When Man intervenes silly things can happen. A classic example was Chairman Mao's decree during the Cultural Revolution that sparrows must be eradicated. As a result there was a plague of other pests that the sparrows had previously controlled. Not often do you get a negative feedback loop destroyed by decree!

Just as no man is an island, so no event is ever totally isolated, though the relationships may be extremely difficult to identify. Chaos theory argues that many complex systems are so finely balanced that a comparatively minor event in one direction rather than another can trigger totally different feedbacks. The example that everyone is talking about these days is El Niño, the ocean current normally flowing north up the coast of Peru. Apparently it takes but a tiny variation in atmospheric pressure on opposite sides of the Pacific Ocean to trigger a reversal of the current. This in turn causes a change in the surface water temperature which can affect the wind direction, and alter the rainfall on the adjacent land.[7] El Niño is blamed for many things from floods in California to droughts in Texas and Chile. So complex are the inter-relations that none of the explanations so far satisfies all the evidence.

This frailty of complex systems is so deeply enshrined in environmental folklore that the story goes that it takes but a butterfly to flap its wings in the steamy depths of the Amazon jungle to alter the course of world events. Whether fantasy or not it conveys a very real message, all summed up in the central message of ecology: 'You can never change only *one* thing'. In every event there are three elements involved. First there is a *cause* which may emerge from outside the immediate system, like an influenza virus entering one's body. This cause eventually has an *effect*. When the effect is noted as a departure from the reference (i.e. healthy) state of the system, that difference becomes the *signal*. One's aching joints or rising temperature or heart beat are all signals that the virus has taken up residence in our bodies and is busy multiplying. The negative feedback that most of us indulge in is to take to our beds leaving the body the energy to fight back.

Nature's signals

Could anyone have guessed in 1970 that CFC gases (a combination of chlorine, fluorine and carbon), which were designed for innocent purposes like pressuring flysprays, could have caused a hole in the ozone layer that lies 20 to 50 kilometres above the earth? Actually, it could probably have been predicted if the question had ever been asked, but it wasn't. It is only in the last fifty years we even came to know there was ozone there, and only more recently that we learned that it could play a critical role in our health. There are about ninety substances that humans have so far created here on Earth that are known to have a similar impact. Even jet engine exhausts have an effect, so when we choose to fly we make our own small contribution to ecological damage.

Ozone is a type of oxygen. Normally oxygen is found in a stable form in which two atoms bond permanently for life, like mating ducks. Ozone comprises three atoms of oxygen. This is not a marriage, but a *ménage à trois*, and as such is rather unstable. Indeed ozone attachments usually last just a few weeks. The union of the three is produced by photo-chemical reactions which are triggered by fine particles such as one finds in smog. Ozone may represent an abnormal situation but it is useful, for in this form oxygen has the ability to screen out ultra-violet radiation, the sort that causes sunburn and skin cancer. However it doesn't take much to split up the ozone trio when an attractive substance like CFC turns up.

The chlorine and third oxygen atom then form a pretty stable bond. The result is that with all the ozone-absorbing substances we are creating, the upper atmosphere is slowly being depleted of ozone, so that life in the open air is becoming more and more dangerous for us.

This effect has been most pronounced in the southern hemisphere, so sunbathing on Bondi beach or Copacabana isn't the fun it used to be. Not only that, but other things such as the growth of crops might be at risk. By autumn 1998 the ozone hole had reached the record size of 26 million square kilometres.[8] This is larger than the total area of South and Central America. And it is still growing.

Now, with the new millennium upon us, we begin to sense that there are signals coming from nature which contain the seeds of disaster for human welfare. For example it is now generally agreed amongst the scientific community that the amount of carbon dioxide we are pushing out as we burn fossil fuels (which are comprised of carbon compounds) is affecting the world's climate and will result, amongst other effects, in the thawing of the polar ice-sheet and a rising sea level. Nature can live with this, but it is certainly a major concern for people living in low-lying terrain and for farmers who may no longer be able to grow crops as they used to. And these are just simple manifestations of what is a rather complex situation that no one claims to fully understand.

The global commons

How do our human demands fit into the wider system? This is well seen through a metaphor provided by the biologist Garret Hardin in a piece he wrote thirty years ago in *Science*, a prestigious weekly American journal. He called it 'The Tragedy of the Commons'. He asked his readers to imagine a situation where several herdsmen shared a common grazing for their animals, much as one still finds in many parts of the world including the Himalayas, the Highlands of Scotland, Lapland and Africa. These pastoralists recognise that a given terrain can support sustainably no more than a certain grazing intensity, and that the number of animals must therefore be limited. By tradition each has a right to graze an equal, fixed number of beasts, the quantity being mutually decided on. Each year they meet to decide their quotas having regard to the state of the pastures. The outcome might be ten cows and twenty sheep, say, per herder.

Now, a rogue herdsman might decide to slyly add one more animal. He would then be better off, and he might argue that one extra beast amongst hundreds could scarcely affect the land's overall productivity, so his fellow herdsmen would not really lose out. This is good competitive thinking on the rogue's part, straight out of a business management school. But if all herdsmen thought like that, the result would be over-grazing and all would eventually suffer a reduced yield: the consequence of greed! What happens here is that the signal is suppressed. It will only be noted when in due course the pasture is seen to be over-grazed.

Would that this were just a theoretical example, but it is happening today in Mongolia. With the fall of the Communist state, Mongolian herders have returned to the free life of the steppes, where they raise cattle on the immense grasslands. There being no agreement on the common rights, animals have numbers soared, reputedly attaining 33 milliion by 2000. Grazing is ruined. Animals are dying. The UN has sent out a call for aid to help keep alive starving nomadic farmers. An even more tragic case is that of Greenland hunters who reduced the world's largest tern colony from 80,000 breeding pairs to 5000 by 1996 and to none by 2000.[9] Yet these birds are part of their life-support system.

It is easy to think of parallel instances. The greedy child who eats more than her share of the cake at a party. The person who parks his car in the bus lane at rush hour. The householder who burns coal in a smokeless zone. The yachtsman who throws plastic matter over the side of the boat, thereby eventually adding to the accumulated detritus on beaches. These are but petty instances. In the interests of competition companies and countries do much worse things on a much larger scale. Saddam Hussein bombed and set fire to Kuwaiti oilfields, generating huge amounts of smoke and carbon dioxide to no useful end. The western developed countries contribute the vast majority of the world's pollution, and consume the major proportion of the world's non-renewable and highly valuable fossil fuels like oil and natural gas. And the USA refused at the Hague conference on emissions in 2000 to meet the requirements laid down by the Kyoto protocol of 1997, a position that President Bush maintained at the 2001 Bonn conference which did achieve some agreement.

The tragedy of the commons lingers on although to some extent Hardin's message has got through to governments. A start was made in 1979, when an international convention of governments met in Montreal to agree on the phasing out of CFC gases, mentioned earlier. However, while the signatories to the CFC protocol may have passed the necessary laws in their own countries, a black market is now flourishing. The illegal marketing of ozone-depleting substances is prevalent in countries like Russia, China and India (the Montreal protocol allows China to produce recycled CFCs for domestic purposes). Despite government attempts to reduce output illegal dealers, aided by loopholes in the system, have falsified documents which make new material appear to be recycled. In the USA a task force on illegal CFCs resulted in the seizure of ten thousand tonnes in 1999.

Hardin believed that in a world of (now) six billion individual human beings, all (in theory) intent on maximising their own personal welfare and with such awesome power to consume, the tragedy of the commons was being collectively re-created on a global scale. In other words sooner rather than later we must mutually decide what is the grazing potential, as it were, of our planet Earth: that is, the durable level of development.

There are some encouraging signs, despite the USA's withdrawal (temporary it is sincerely to be hoped). After much haggling at the 2001 Bonn inter-governmental conference on atmospheric emissions, the nations agreed on some modest reduction targets mainly by the western developed economies. However at this meeting governmental representatives were at pains to negotiate targets that would still allow for economic expansion – that allowed positive feedback to prevail. The competitive free market thus sits uneasily side by side with the Hardin parable, for it espouses competition, whereas the parable suggests the need for consensus and stability. The free market assumes an infinitely expandable economy. The parable focuses on the limited physical potential of the system. Later on we shall consider whether the two can be mutually compatible. First we look more closely at the meaning of money.

Notes

1   *Gaia Takes Flight*, J. Lovelock, 1992, Earthwatch, Washington DC.
2   This a long-term trade cycle identified by the Russian economist N.D. Kondratieff.
3   It is quite possible in an unrestricted market for one firm to defeat all others and create a monopoly and then set its prices irrespective of demand.
4   Dana Meadows was a co-author of the seminal book *The Limits to Growth* published in 1972. Prior to her death in 2001 she was the editor of a quarterly newsletter of the International Network of Resource Information Centres (INRIC) known as the *Balaton Bulletin* (comment circulated on 3/12/98).
5   *When Corporations Rule the World,* D.C. Korten, Earthscan, 1995, London.
6   Actually in money of the day it will always rise due to inflation, but in real terms will peak.
7   *Climate Process and Change*, Edward Bryant, 1997, p 68, Cambridge UniversityPress.
8   *The Chemical Engineer* (Journal of the UK Institution of Chemical Engineers), 22/10/98, p8.
9   *Arctic Bulletin*, No. 4, 2001, p 21.

4

Money as a concept

Most people have a magnified impression of the intelligence of those who live in intimate association with large sums of money. This is an erroneous belief, as the ultimate reckoning so readily reveals.
J.K. GALBRAITH, 1995

Most people accept that the world is finite; of a certain mass, a certain volume, containing a limited number of elements. It follows that if we use up some of these finite resources, then there will be less left for future generations. Money is quite different. All the time there is more and more of it. How can this be? The answer is quite simple. Since money is a concept, an abstraction, whose amount is limited only by human creativity there is no physical impediment to its creation. How strange that we should base our economic management, both personal and national, on something that is not real. Yet we know only too well from experience that money is power, and taken very seriously by one and all. An enormous number of people gain their incomes from handling and accounting for money. It plays a huge, if not dominating, role in most people's lives.

In one dictionary of quotations only love elicits more entries than money. Karl Marx thought it 'alienated the essence of Man's work'. The lure and power of money have a long history. As far back as the first century BC, Publius Syrus observed that 'Money alone sets the world in motion'. St Paul, in his epistle to Timothy,[1] was less enthusiastic; 'the love of money is the root of all evil'. Since a lot of people believe in money, probably more than those who believe in God, there must surely be something more to it than a mere abstraction. After all, that bank note in your pocket will persuade a vendor to part with his goods. And he in turn knows he can then use it to buy something he wants, unless that note happens to be a 1996 rouble or a 1919 Deutschmark, when it took a barrow load to pay for a meal.

So what's the trick with money?

At one time money was real and tangible, usually gold and silver and marketed as ducats, doubloons, sovereigns and so forth. Digging these hard-to-find and thus precious elements out of the soil was one way to riches. Piracy and plunder were easier and quicker. The Spanish conquistadors of Peru and Ecuador were lured by Inca gold as much as by the prospect of land. The tragedy is that a vast array of Inca gold objects, often of great beauty, were simply melted down. In those days the money supply was limited by the amount of gold and silver in circulation. Ironically, though gold represented wealth, it was not of itself the means of wealth creation. And so it remains to this day.

As a form of cash gold was not very convenient. Lugging sacks of heavy metal around is tedious and an invitation to robbers and pirates. The solution was to use some other token to represent gold. Provided one could trust that it could always be exchanged for the real thing, this was a reasonable procedure. Older readers will remember when a Bank of England or US Treasury note bore the words 'promise to pay the bearer on demand … gold'. For token money to work one needs an ordered society and a government willing and able to crack down on counterfeiters. That sort of money was much more convenient. One could swap tokens instead of bartering one cow for fifty hens and three bushels of wheat, when all you might want was one bushel of wheat and two hens.

Though no one knows for sure when human ingenuity first thought up money it did circulate for a while in ancient China and Egypt and was re-invented by the Lydians in what is now Turkey. All sorts of things were used as monetary tokens. Cowrie shells and human skulls were popular in Africa. Paper money circulated in the eleventh-century China. But it took the thirteenth-century oriental potentate and tyrant Kubla Khan to find out how truly to exploit the invention of money, and make it a system for self-enrichment.

Marco Polo records in Samuel Purchas' translation, 'The money of the great Kan is not made of gold and silver or other metall, but they take the middle barke from the Mulberrie Tree, and this they make firme, and cut it into divers and round pieces, great and little, and imprint the Kings mark thereon. Of this matter therefore, the Emperor causeth an huge masse of money to bee made in the Citie of Cambalu, which sufficeth for the whole Empire: and no man under paine of death may lawfully coine any other, or spend any other money, or refuse it in all his Kingdomes and Countries. Nor any comming from another Kingdome, dare spend any other money in the Empire of the great Kan. Whereby it cometh to passe, that Merchants often coming from farre remote Countries and Regions unto the Citie of Cambalu bring with them gold and silver, pearle and precious stones and receive the Kings money for them. And because this money is not received in their Countries they change it againe in the Empire of the great Kan for merchandise, which they carrie away with them… Wherefore, there is not a King to be found in all the world, who exceedeth him in Treasure'.

One has to hand it to the old fellow. He really knew how to screw the trading classes and build up his assets. His money was legal tender only in his own kingdom; it was worthless beyond. The only way foreign merchants could extract the value of their sales was by buying goods in the Khan's lands. The technique of the wily Khan has re-surfaced today where supermarkets and airlines offer points and airmiles which must then be spent in their own stores or aeroplanes.

Paper money was not universally accepted till well into the Victorian era. Montesquieu,writing in 1797, pointed out that *only* rare metal could act as a legitimate measure of value. 'Could this be done by the leaves or bark of trees? No. Why? Because little labour was necessary to procure them, and being of no use in themselves, they would not be received in exchange for that which it required the exertion of industry to procure'. Here is a hint of a labour theory of money, of which more anon. Until relatively recently ordinary people were suspicious of paper money, preferring to hoard such wealth as they had in some tangible form that enjoyed universal appeal like gold, silver and precious stones. Many a mattress was ripped open to serve as a hiding place.

What a waste all this effort to extract gold has been. Gold has little intrinsic value, though its physical properties are uncommon. It is dense, malleable, chemically inactive and so corrosion resistant, and it has a pleasing sheen. One can say the same of platinum, titanium or palladium. Its value as a token is that it is humanly desired, yet to a great extent this is hyped.

The weakness of holding gold as money is that in itself it cannot do anything. It cannot make fertilisers, or manufacture cars. Nor can it propel an aeroplane through the sky any more than can a bank note or a circle of mulberry bark. It seems rather absurd that we mine gold ore, purify it, and then put it into some bank vault. It would be less trouble, and would have altered the world's wealth not one whit, had it been left in the ground! How many miners have died extracting gold? In South Africa the figure is more than 50,000 in the twentieth century alone. If only electronic money had been invented sooner! The pointlessness of gold as a store of wealth is only just beginning to be realised. Several western governments have recently sold some of their country's gold reserves, accepting in lieu currency of another country.

The real wealth of a nation is in its manufacturing potential and educated human resources. In Alice Walker's poem *We Alone*:

> *We alone can devalue gold*
> *by not caring*
> *if it falls or rises*
> *in the market place.*

Wherever there is gold there is a chain, you know
and if your chain is gold
so much the worse for you.
Feathers, shells
and sea-shaped stones
are all as rare.
This could be our revolution:
To love what is plentiful
as much as what's scarce.[2]

The early monetary tokens had only a limited regional validity. It is doubtful if in mediaeval Europe a dried skull or a circle of mulberry bark would have been accepted in exchange for even a loaf of bread. Now a euro is acceptable to 300 million Europeans, and the American dollar to most of the world.

Money is now created independently of true wealth creation; for example when credit card debt is transformed into a mortgage on a home. This situation has been exacerbated by the development of financial derivatives (of which more later). The rot started with credit. The ancient Greeks are said to have been the first to pull off this one. It is 300 BC. Imagine an agricultural trader planning to travel from Athens to Alexandria with a view to buying a ship-load of cheap wheat, which he can then sell to the local bakers at a profit. At this time the only tokens widely acceptable are gold and silver. Imagine lugging all that weight around! To pay for 100 tonnes of wheat will require about 10 kilograms of gold. There are many risks in carrying it: robbers, shipwreck and the temptations of the flesh in far parts. So he lodges his gold with a reliable chap who 'banks' it on a shelf in his cellar, and issues a slip of papyrus bearing a written receipt. The fact that the banker fellow is well known and respected, even as far away as Egypt, means this receipt is as good as gold. It is light to carry and almost useless to a robber or a tempting houri. There is a small charge for this. In due course the receipt finds its way back to the Greek banker who hands over the gold to whoever tenders the original receipt. All this calls for a great deal of trust, but then without trust there is no civilisation.

After a while it occurred to Greek bankers that they could issue these credit notes without someone actually first depositing an equivalent collateral in gold, for by the time the note was presented for payment, other depositors would have banked their gold: there was always some gold on the 'bank'. Thus the bankers could issue more credit notes than they needed gold to back them. One effect was to put more purchasing power into circulation than was represented by the gold stored on the 'banks'. This increase in monetary tokens stimulated trade. It made the bankers rich, and the traders' lives easier. It represented a significant shift in power from kings and despots to merchants and bankers. Today the pinnacle of that power rests in the hands of people like the chairman of the Federal Reserve in Washington and the head of the new European bank upon whose good sense and commitment much depends.

If by any unhappy twist of fate more letters of credit were simultaneously presented than there was gold on the banks there was trouble. Today this is called a run on the bank. So it pays bankers to be prudent and not too greedy. To be successful in the long run, it is important to have an unblemished reputation. It will not surprise the cynical reader that many banks have over-played their hands, and gone bust when they have lent too much and too many depositors at one time have wanted their cash back, as happened in the great depression in the USA in the 1930s when one in five US banks folded. Leaving bankers in sole charge of credit is like letting children into a sweetie factory.

The next logical step for the bankers was to lend money. For a fee, known now as interest, the banker would issue credit even though again no gold or silver had been deposited to back it up. If this credit was banked with the issuing banker, or paid to someone who also banked with him, then the banker did rather well out of it. He received interest, but lost no capital. If the credit was banked with another banker, the effect was to further increase the money in circulation. This worked fine as long as not too many people presented notes for payment at any one time and the money was being put to good productive use. The ratio of credit issued to monetary reserves is known today as the reserve ratio, only gold is no longer used.

The great virtue of this system is that it greases the wheels of economic expansion. The great danger is that money becomes diluted and unreliable, as is increasingly happening. The Earl of Caithness speaking in a House of Lords debate on the economy ended his speech with, 'The next government must grasp the nettle, accept their responsibility for controlling the money and change from our debt-based monetary system. My lords, will they? If they do not, our money system will break us, and the sorry legacy we are already leaving our children will be a disaster'.[3]

Today national central banks maintain a watchful eye on the commercial banks, and stipulate the required reserve ratios. At least most do. The temptation to print money as a way out of trouble is not unknown amongst governments.[4] Unlike banks, ordinary people are not allowed to create money.

The combination of credit and loans set the world upon a new and fascinating path where the amount of money in circulation bore no relation to the capacity to generate wealth. Indeed, it became no longer possible to know how much wealth there was. The word began to lose its old meaning. Today, if 'wealth' means anything, it means power.

In spite of the stunning success of the invention of credit it declined in medi-aeval Europe, largely because the Roman Catholic Church condemned the practice of usury. Islamic doctrine took the same view. However you cannot keep a good money-making idea down, and it revived in Renaissance Italy in the early fourteenth-century . Soon some Florentine bankers were so rich that they were able to open agencies abroad. The most famous were the Medici family. Banking really took off in 1694 when William Paterson persuaded the king of England that by creating a Bank of England he could more easily pay for his wars.

Gold had long been the bankers' answer. By 1870 most currencies were expressed in terms of a specified weight of gold – the gold standard. The world went off the gold standard in 1914 at the outbreak of the first world war, when money creation on a vast scale was necessary to finance the war effort. This made possible the weapons of destruction, but created no assets. So money lost its value, as patriotic citizens who had bought war bonds eventually found out to their cost. In fact creating money erodes wealth, causing inflation, and reducing the buying power of existing money. It particularly inflates the monetary value of non-reproducible things like oil and land and those products derived from them.

In an effort to stabilise the world's finances after the devastation of the second world war, the gold standard was re-instated at a conference attended by 44 nations at Bretton Woods in New Hampshire in 1944. The value of the US dollar was set at thirty-five to the ounce (28.4 g) of gold. All the signatory governments were to peg their currencies to gold, and by implication to the dollar. For those then enjoying the average American income, the monthly wage packet in gold would have weighed three quarters of a pound or a third of a kilogram. Obviously it is impossible to conduct modern life using tangible money.

The gold standard lasted only thirty-five years. Very cleverly, in 1979, the US government without warning doubled the dollar price of gold overnight. In so doing it halved the US international debt! Today the world has no standard against which to value money. Just imagine if there were no international standard for length or weight; that each nation chose its own value for the metre, and allowed it to change year by year. Every currency is a creature of every other in the merry-go-round of the world's financial markets. Though the US dollar is the most widely respected and widely held currency, its value vis-à-vis others varies hourly.

Money as a measure of value

'Economics is a science which treats phenomena from the standpoint of price' according to one commentator.[5] Monetary value lies in opinion, or rather two opinions; that of the seller and that of the buyer. The price of a good is arrived at by a process that evenly distributes disappointment.

Valuing money through opinion has two disadvantages. Firstly, opinions change over time and space. You might offer five pounds for your friend's tie today, but by next week you might have lost interest. Opinions arise from human perceptions that may or may not be grounded in reality, and often change unpredictably. Nothing reveals this more starkly than the stock market, driven as it is by a mixture of hope, greed and opportunism. This fickle quality in human behaviour is a serious problem for economists seeking to forecast the evolution of the economy. Their approach is to research into people's purchasing habits (in the mass) and examine how they respond to price changes (*demand elasticity*), and then project these into the future. The nub of the problem is guessing how long into the future the resulting coefficients are valid. Some key prices, such as those of energy resources, cannot be forecast at all.

The second disadvantage of money, as an opinion, is that it has no international standard. Each nation sets up its own currency, and the coefficients relating these (the exchange rates) vary considerably, and often quickly. Now the collective opinion of a large number of people interacting in the market place does indeed arrive at a momentary value for one commodity in terms of one specific currency. The perceived (marginal) utility of a product or service will determine its marketable price or *exchange value*. This in turn will be affected by the purchasing power of the consumers in the market. It is not unusual to find identical products to be valued at different prices according to the relative affluence of the available consumers. A Picasso drawing for sale on the Left Bank in Paris will fetch more than in the street markets of South America. It is noteworthy that for bulk manufactured commodities like grain, metals, cement or fertilisers, which are made in much the same way the world over and enjoy no artistic or scarcity value, the exchange value is proportional to the total energy embodied in the manufacture of the product.[6] This has led some people to put forward an energy theory of value. This is anathema to the economist.

Money supply

If money is simply an abstract human invention, why do we not just make more of it, so we would all be richer? Of course we know the answer to that absurd proposition – more money around simply dilutes the purchasing power of existing money. But it *is* necessary to create it. The exchanges that take place among the roughly six billion individuals on this planet are almost entirely carried out using money. If today the amount (in technical language the *money supply*) were the same as in St Paul's time trade would be impossible. The supply has to expand with economic activity.

The money that goes round and round our economies does so at a varying rate, called the velocity of circulation. Monetarists offer the following relationship:

General price level equals money supply multiplied by velocity of circulation divided by ouput, or as an equation:

general price level = (money supply * velocity of circulation) / output

It follows that if the money supply or velocity goes up more than output so does the price level; that is, inflation takes place. The American economists Charles Hall, Cutler Cleveland and Robert Kaufmann adapted this equation to show the link between money supply, prices and the energy consumption in the economy.[7] Pointing out that there was a statistical link between energy use and GDP, they modified the monetarist equation to:

general price level = (money supply * velocity of circulation of money)/ (energy use * efficiency)

where 'efficiency' is interpreted as the technological efficiency with which a unit of energy is usefully deployed. This is a bit vague, and in the next chapter we shall introduce a more rigorous interpretation. No doubt to their joy, the statistical data showed that their equation revealed an excellent correlation with the consumer price index for the US economy over ninety years! To quote them 'the ratio of money supply to energy consumption explains 99% of the level of the US consumer price index'. For those who would like to see the maths, see the appendix to Chapter 5, but not till you have read that chapter.

Can money measure output and welfare?

Economic output is conventionally measured as the sum of all values exchanged, called the gross domestic product or GDP. The same number is arrived at (in principle, as there are many inevitable errors in such accounting) by adding up everyone's income. This procedure only includes activities where money changes hands. A housewife, who labours for her family, is not included. But a paid housekeeper is. If she subsequently marries her employer GDP is reduced by the amount of her previous wages. Indeed GDP masks so much vital information as to be a poor indicator of the welfare of a nation. GDP is expressed in a monetary unit, and since inflation erodes money's buying power, it has to be stated in the currency of the day. For example in 1998 the average Swiss income was 28,000 Swiss francs while in the UK it was £11,000. To compare the average material welfare of the citizens of one country with that of another economists use the concept of *purchasing power parity*, that is to say what you can buy with your money. By this measure the Swiss are thought to be 36% better off. Has this any meaning in terms of material welfare or quality of life? Switzerland gives an impression of calm, the UK of a frenetic society. People in the UK work longer hours than any others in Europe. But not all Britons want to live in Switzerland or vice versa.

It used to be held that GDP per head was the true measure of welfare. The higher and faster it rose, the better things were supposed to be. Today, many disagree. What GDP measures is activity, much of which may be pointless. For example when bus services are de-regulated, there are more buses using more fuel, but carrying fewer passengers per bus. More activity, indeed. But activity reflects neither efficiency[8] nor quality of life.

A topical example of how this form of accountancy can mislead is to imagine that all speed limits on the roads have been suspended. There would then be a higher rate of accidents, thereby incurring both medical and car repair activities. This would lead to a rise in GDP, but as some of the workforce would be languishing in hospital, output might well be down! Recently an electricity company complained that its lower profits were due to a warm winter. This would, in its small way, also diminish the GDP. In a bizarre comment, one economic journalist commented that the reconstruction needed in the aftermath of the Iraqi invasion of Kuwait provided exceptional opportunities for increased economic activity. Is this an argument in favour of more war?

The American economist Herman Daly has offered a measure of welfare that better reflects quality of life. He calls it the *Index of Sustainable Economic Welfare* (ISEW). This index is a combination of a subjective, though in our view well chosen, set of indicators. It shows that in some countries where the GDP has been steadily rising, their ISEW has not. However it is always difficult to defend an index whose components are given weightings that depend on human value judgements. Moreover the indices chosen are all couched in monetary units.

Money as power

The reader can be excused for thinking that this chapter has not got very far in explaining the meaning of money, but there are still a couple of aspects of the monetary system that remain to be be examined. The first is that most of us are in thrall to money; not our own, but that commanded by others. Money talks. Money is power. The command of money provides a means to implement one's desires. A rich person can impose his or her will, buy the best advice, lobby the politicians, be host to useful people. Here we find a very positive feedback loop; the rich tend to become richer. Clearly, if democratic power is to be restored to society, then some negative feedback loops need to be legislated. Professor Ian Angell of the London School of Economics and the American journalist Thomas Friedman[9] tell us that nothing can be done. Resistance is futile. The 'electronic herd', as Friedman calls the rich speculators, will sweep all before them. We must not, he advises, be morally distracted by the inequality, environmental destruction, lack of employment, economic insecurity and the loss of cultural diversity that keeping in with the herd will demand; otherwise you too, dear reader, will be left behind. This attitude begs the question: 'how much inequality can a democracy sustain?' Sooner or later something will upset the monetary apple-cart.

Easy money

Nothing is more likely to precipitate revolution than the growing disparity between rich and poor. This refers not merely to the huge salaries that corporate executives award their peers, a process of mutual back-rubbing, but of the enormous amounts of money that can be made out of money. No need to go to the bother of producing something tangible or providing a service like a good restaurant. This activity is known as the 'financial services industry'. What cheek! Industry is about producing something. The 'finance industry' produces nothing.[10] What it does is to cream off a bit of our hard-won earnings as they pass over the desks of financial advisers, there to emerge as endowment insurances, units trusts, portfolio management agreements, mortgages, pension provisions and so on. To these advisors money must indeed have the illusion of reality. They claim to be able to make your savings grow. Their investment opinions, though, have about as much durability as a fireguard made of chocolate. William Sherden examined the market gurus of the United States and came to the conclusion that fund managers consistently failed to beat the market.[11] It is not coyness, but government regulation, that obliges them to insert the small print that says 'investments can fall as well as gain in value'. Indeed! In the good times, the financial advisers make a bit for you and a bit for themselves. In the bad times they still make a bit for themselves, but your equity may decline. This is entirely contrary to the principle of the free market where it is recognised that risk and profit go hand in hand. These people take no risks; their commissions are guaranteed. Even worse are the 'analysts', upon whose advice investors pledge their funds. Their unrelenting optimism temporarily pushes up stock prices, which then cannot be sustained, and investors bear the loss. As the headline in the *New York Times* put it (about analysts), 'Today salesmanship takes precedence over research'.[12]

Nonetheless these people do have a role to play in our modern society, for not everyone can manage their own savings. One would wish that they paid themselves a little less and returned to their clients a little more. Still, enough of carping. As the successful investor George Soros[13] comments, 'Financial markets are inherently unstable'. So we should not expect too much rigour from the so-called financial experts.[14]

But this easy money is nothing compared to the money game, where the world is held to ransom by margin traders. True, huge risks have to be taken, but it is usually with other people's money. This game is called 'financial derivatives'. These include futures and option trading. First, futures. There is a valuable side to the futures market in stabilising commodity prices. For example a chocolate manufacturer must be sure of a sustained supply of cocoa. This is grown in tropical countries like the Ivory Coast, Brazil and Indonesia, none notable for stable currencies. In addition, all sorts of unexpected events can affect the cocoa harvest, and thus the price of cocoa. So the manufacturer strikes a deal with a futures dealer that at some specified time in the future he will be able to buy a given amount of cocoa at an agreed fixed price. As far as the manufacturer is concerned the stability of supply is well worth the premium paid. The speculator may win or lose, but has his money up front. In this game there are always risk takers and risk makers.

But option trading is where the gambling instinct can really express itself. These activities have exploded to the point where the money that passes in one day through the London International Financial Futures and Options Exchange (LIFFE) and Eurex in Frankfurt is as great as that used to finance all the world's trade in a whole year. Currency options offer the most excitement where huge gains and losses are possible on trivial margins. Nick Leeson, a trader for Barings Bank in Singapore made some bad guesses and cost his company £600m. He bankrupted Barings and was jailed.[15] If he had guessed rightly he would have been a millionaire and promoted. In 1992 George Soros, the Hungarian American who runs the Quantum fund in New York, bet on the weakness of the pound sterling. Such was the size of his bet – a billion pounds – that he influenced the market. The pound fell 14 per cent, and Soros made a killing. To do him justice most of that went in philanthropic endowments to eastern Europe.

One buys an *option* to exchange one currency (or bond or share) for another at some future specified date at a specified price, called the *exercise* price. This will happen only if one party to the contract (either the prospective buyer or the prospective seller) wants to go ahead with the sale. A *call* option is when the buyer has the right to decide whether or not the sale occurs; a *put* option is when the seller decides.

The holder of an option pays a premium for these valuable rights. The premium depends on several things, but mostly on the risk. Incidentally a domestic house mortgage is a form of option trading. If you have a fixed rate mortgage, and the price of borrowing drops, you can exercise your option to sell out, and borrow elsewhere.

There is nothing illegal in all this. But because the flows are through international financial markets they are outside the control of any national government or international agency. Option trading was at the root of the 1998 Asian crisis.

It's only money – an experiment

To do this experiment rigorously you need four items. They are a bank note of any denomination or currency, a match, some sort of fireproof pincers and a letter-weighing scale. If you lack the latter, try the post office.

Now imagine you are on a desert island with a wallet full of bank notes. In this environment they have no value. However they do represent a source of heat, and you are dying for a cup of hot coffee. So why not burn the bank notes? Well, how much heat can you expect?

Weigh the bank note. Hold one corner by the pincer. Light the match and apply it to the opposite corner of the note. Observe that it burns like any other piece of paper, because that is all it is – paper.

You are now burning a token representing money. When the note is completely burnt away reflect on the consequences. Here are some:

1. The heat generated by the combustion is equal to the weight in grams of the banknote times 0.18 MJ. This might furnish a demi-tasse of tepid coffee.

2. The energy to make the bank note was about three times as much as it yielded on combustion. This represents the only burden on the world's resources of issuing this token.

3. Whoever issued the note in the first place has unwittingly become richer, since the debt represented by this note need never be repaid.

4. Your own purchasing power (were you ever to return to civilisation) has been reduced by the nominal value of the note.

5. This energy has been pointlessly dissipated, which if utilised in an engine would have done some useful *work*.

6. Additional carbon dioxide has been released into the atmosphere which is about one and a half times as much as the bank note weighed.

The leaders of the G7 countries have since huffed and puffed that something must be done, but nothing has emerged. Soros himself disapproves of the situation, believing it could undermine the whole capitalist financial system. He comments: 'The explosive growth in derivative instruments holds other dangers. There are so many of them, and some are so esoteric, that the risks involved may not be properly understood even by the most sophisticated of investors. Some appear to be specifically designed to enable institutional investors to take gambles which they would otherwise not be permitted to take.' [16]

The economist James Tobin has put forward the idea of a tax on these transactions (the Tobin tax), to slow down the circulation of this functionless money. The likelihood, unfortunately, is that if it were imposed the entire operation would go off-shore, or onto the Internet (or possibly off-planet!).

Tucked in here is the joker in the pack; expert systems. These are computer models designed by an 'expert' to enable less expert people come to a decision. The model contains a set of rules (algorithms) which are based on a study of the system behaviour. For example, an expert system on wheat trading will deliver certain conclusions if the user types into the computer his or her guesses about future demand. The trouble with this sort of facility is that a lot of wheat traders will use the same or similar models. These models are designed to work in a competitive market, not one chasing its own tail. If there is a rumour about some factor in the market changing, everyone will plug in the same change, in effect creating a positive feedback which will cause a violent surge in price up or down. It may truly be a case of the blind leading the blind. Professor John Gray in his book *False Dawn*[17] remarks: 'The enormous, practically unknowable virtual economy of financial derivatives enhances the risks of systemic crash'.

Money as decision

So at last we come to deal with the real meaning of money. To do so we have to separate the concept of money from the physical reality of the biosphere upon which our welfare truly depends. It is not easy to get this idea over because we are all brought up in a totally money-orientated world; its credo is that if you've enough money the world is your oyster. So let us approach this important intellectual step by way of an example.

Imagine you have a concession to extract oil from some corner of the earth's surface. You bore your well, and out comes the oil. Nature, bountiful as always, has not demanded any payment for this. As far as she is concerned it is free. You sell the oil and after deducting costs make a profit. But if the oil is free, what are these costs? First there is the rent of the land (for which nature also made no charge), then the salaries and wages of the people working for you and the equipment you have to buy, all of which costs money. The equipment comprises rigs, trucks and all manner of hardware. The price of this, in turn, takes into account all the wages and salaries of their manufacture, together with the human effort of extracting and refining the metals and other materials used. The ultimate source of all materials is, however, the Earth, that is to say nature, which makes no charge at all. In other words the costs, in money, of extracting the oil comprise only present and past labour costs. Some of these may have been incurred in another country or at an earlier time. They tend to be higher if one is recruiting educated labour such as managers and engineers. Every person involved in this tortuous chain of events from the lowliest labourer to the skilled professional are hired for one reason and one reason alone: *their ability to make decisions*. The payment they receive or have received is a relative payment not an absolute one, for money has no absolute value. Thus a manual worker whose decision role is small receives a fraction of the payment of a manager. The manager can command many times as many goods and services (ignoring tax for the moment) as the labourer.

This is not quite the old labour theory of value espoused by Karl Marx and David Ricardo. That has been discredited in the eyes of most modern economists for the reason that it does not take into account the capital and primary resources that also go into production. In the approach presented above, however, we have iterated back through the entire network to identify those human interventions that made the final output possible. Those interventions – decisions, as we prefer to label them – represent the *management* of nature's resources which calls for human effort, intelligence and time. Payment for our efforts is given not just in accordance with the perceived value of our contribution as judged by the marketplace, but in proportion to average price level. An executive in the USA or India may have an income that can command the labour of ten labourers in their own region, but an Indian executive on an Indian salary visiting the USA could never match that buying power. The two inputs, human and those provided by nature, are essentially different. The human input can be reflected in monetary terms. Nature's input cannot. That is why money means decision.

Another example may help. Consider a tractor driver who has been asked to plough a field. He is not expected to employ his own strength for the purpose of turning the soil. His role is to control the tractor, and *decide* where it goes. The tractor pulls the plough. The power required is provided by an engine, fuelled by some energy source like diesel fuel. The actual physical work of dragging the plough through the soil is obtained by the combustion of the fuel in the engine. At the end of the job the ploughman receives a monetary wage. The world's non-renewable energy stores are depleted that little bit further, but there is nothing in the tractor-man's payment that encompasses that. Wages cannot incorporate natural resources.

It is unlikely that a paraplegic whose strength could not even turn the tractor's steering wheel would be employed as a tractor driver for the reason that tractors do not yet work on remote control. Still, it is not impossible for this to happen in the future. Individuals sitting in their chairs might one day, in the manner of the paralysed physicist Stephen Hawkins, come to manipulate the computer that controls the signals sent to the tractor. Only a little more capital (and hence energy) would be involved. The point to take in here is that since the time of subsistence farming (which still exists in parts of the world) machines have gradually taken over the role of human labour to the point where in the modern economy the contribution of people as a source of labour rather than decision-making is negligible. How negligible is revealed in Chapter 6.

If money represents only human decision-making, then the price of something reflects both the quantity and perceived quality of the decision-making required to produce it. Executive officers of large corporations can command salaries of the order of millions a year. Their girl Fridays are paid less because their task is considered to be relatively simple. To repeat, the value put upon one person's time is relative to that of others. Every currency, too, is relative to every other. There is not and cannot ever be an absolute standard unit of money. But even more important again, money cannot quantify nature's contribution.

How does capital fit into this picture of money? It is simply the cumulative decision cost of producing something which is not consumed at once, but is installed, and greases the means of using labour effectively. The reason that living standards can rise is that the decision potential of an educated labour force, coupled to capital investment, is able to produce more physical or service output per unit of decision time. All the time nature is providing the physical raw materials for free. Because of this the legally enforced ownership or right of control of mineral resources is extremely highly valued. Generally governments arrogate it to themselves and charge a royalty. Needless to say the money doesn't go to nature, which doesn't have a bank account, and anyway has no inherent greed.

If money cannot quantify nature's contribution to human welfare is there anything that can? This is the subject of the following chapter.

Notes

1   Timothy 1 6:10

2   *We Alone*, Alice Walker, 1992 in the anthology *Her Blue Body: Everything we Know*, Women's Press, London

3   *Hansard*, 578, 68, columns 1869-1871 (5th March, 1997).

4   In the *The Management of Government Debt*: 'Government financing policy is fundamentally linked to monetary policy. If the budget deficit could be covered simply by printing money with no harmful effects on the rest of the economy, it would make sense for the government to use this means. But it is widely accepted that the monetary consequences of such financing would be harmful to the economy', 1996 (5 May) Bank of England, Centre for Banking Studies, first para, section 3 on co-ordination of monetary policy.

5   *Europe 1992 and the Developing World*, M. Davenport, 1986, Croom Helm, London

6 *Energy and Value*, P. Roberts, 1982, Energy Policy, 10: 171-180

7 *Energy and Resource Quality,* C.A.S. Hall, C.J. Cleveland and R Kaufmann, 1986, p61, John Wiley, New York.

8 Efficiency is a much abused word with many interpretations. Consider the efficiency of a bus service. From the travellers' point of view it is one that arrives within moments of reaching the bus stop. To the operator it is one in which the bus is full of paying passengers. Economic efficiency and resource efficiency are quite different things.

9 *The Lexus and the Olive Tree,* T. Friedman, 1999, Farrar Strauss Giroux, New York.

10 The misuse of the word 'industry' is now quite widespread. One comes across 'the prostitution industry', 'the prison industry', 'the pensions industry'!

11 *The Fortune Sellers,* William A. Sherden, 1998, John Wiley, New York.

12 *New York Times* service 2/01/2001.

13 *Soros on Soros,* G. Soros, 1995, John Wiley, New York.

14 William Sherden, in his book *The Fortune Sellers*, found that the status of stock market forecasters was largely myth. Examining one prominent and much respected market guru, he found that a better result might have been had by tossing a coin!

15 The story is captured in the film *RogueTrader.*

16 Soros, ibid, pp313-4.

17 *False Dawn*, J. Gray, 1998, Granta, London..

5

Bringing nature into the equation

Man conquers nature by obeying her.
FRANCIS BACON

While it is perfectly obvious that we cannot live without nature's bounty of air, water, mineral resources and so forth, how can they be evaluated in a way that takes account of their finite nature? In short how do we incorporate them into the human economic equation. As we averred in Chapter 4, money cannot do it. Nature levies no monetary charge. She is without human motivation and having no bank account cannot accumulate monetary wealth. Indeed, nature is wealth. But the vital point is that she does not recognise the human-made convention of ownership of natural resources and land.

Environmental economists maintain that they can and do incorporate the environment into the economic equation. There are innumerable pages in the academic economic literature devoted to the topic. Perhaps one of the most ambitious is the 1997[1] article in the prestigious science journal *Nature* in which a group of ecologically minded economists, ecologists, geographers and agriculturists explained how they valued the world's eco-system and natural capital. Their figure was 33 trillion US dollars! This was about twice the formal world gross domestic product at that time. While such a calculation serves to remind one that nature does make a huge contribution to our welfare it falls into the trap of treating it as if it espoused a human value system. It is the same trap that resulted in one recent study, best forgotten, which valued the life of a US citizen at one million dollars while that of a Bangladeshi is valued at nine thousand. Nature's role in our lives is physical, biological and aesthetic, not monetary.

The phrase 'natural' capital is in distinction to human-made or manufactured capital (hereafter called HMC). It is an apt and felicitous description, for it conveys the impression of a structure and of a stock which if used is depleted. Since HMC consists of physical entities like buildings, bridges, railways, factories and so forth, that are all manufactured out of materials whose sole source is the biosphere, it follows that HMC is not only derived from natural capital, but can *only* be derived from natural capital. However since all extraction and manufacturing processes inevitably create some waste, more natural capital has to be extracted than finishes up in HMC. The totality of HMC that we humans can ultimately make is limited by our access to natural capital.

That said, there is an awful lot of it to hand. Nonetheless whatever the prevailing dogma it cannot be denied that any economic process that uses *non-renewable* natural capital inevitably depletes it. Some economists have proposed that the monetary value of this depletion be deducted from GDP to arrive at a 'true' national product. It is a nice idea, but subject to enormous uncertainty, for how does one appropriately value something in human terms that nature offers for free, using a unit of account which varies from moment to moment? This procedure has nevertheless led to what are known as *resource accounts*.

Natural capital falls into three categories: renewable, recyclable and non-renewable (or depletable). These important distinctions will be discussed in Chapter 6, but in what follows bear in mind that fossil energy resources are the principal forms of depletable natural capital.

The first approach of the economists in handling the effect of using up depletable natural capital was to propose a *constant capital rule:* that when the *value* of the natural capital consumed in the process of production is deducted from the *value* of the resulting HMC then, if the net sum is constant or increasing, the system may be considered 'sustainable'. At first sight this seems eminently plausible. But since human effort goes into creating HMC, and such effort requires monetary payment, the monetary value of the resulting human-made capital is bound to exceed the price of the raw materials used in its manufacture. Thus this sum can only ever be positive. Interpreted in such a way sustainability is guaranteed!

Many economists accept the flaws in this approach, for it assumes all forms of capital (HMC, human and natural) are mutually interchangeable, which is manifestly not the case; try substituting human beings for petrol to propel your car. Recognising that flaw economists, with (we assume) academic humour, call this rule *weak sustainability* and go on to propose *strong sustainability.* This takes account of the fact that certain critical forms of natural capital cannot be substituted for. But once again the monetary value of HMC is always going to be higher than the monetary value of the energy resources thereby depleted in making it, because it includes not only the worth attached to the energy source by conventional economic valuation, but the additional decision cost of the labour used to make the HMC.

The reality of the situation becomes clearer if one looks at *strong sustainability* in physical rather than monetary terms.

Here is an example. Consider the manufacture and use of a wind turbine designed to generate electricity. The wind is free. However one has first to build the turbine. This is human-made capital, and thus originates from natural capital of which part will be depletable, like the oil or coal energy used up in its manufacture. There is no depletion of fuel to drive the turbine for the wind blows whether used or not, nor is there a monetary cost because human beings have not yet found a way of 'owning' the wind (and let us hope they never do). Like all machines, it will have a limited life; say 20 years.

We now apply a life-cycle analysis (also known as a net energy analysis). This is a well developed methodology[2] whose details need not concern us here. The turbine will be a physically sustainable investment if the energy generated over its lifetime exceeds the energy initially invested in its manufacture. However if it only just equalled that initial energy investment it would serve no purpose. It would be as pointless as a farmer's grain yield providing just enough seed for next year's planting but no more. A durable system must generate a surplus. As it turns out a typical wind turbine does that. Working out the numbers for a one-kilowatt turbine we find:

• the energy required to build the turbine is 5 barrels oil equivalent (these figures are approximate).

• the likely electricity generated over 20 years will be 44,000 kWh (domestic 'units').[3]

• the time to pay back the original energy investment in the turbine is 1.5 years.

Thus the turbine is physically sustainable because for an initial investment of 5 barrels (36GJ) of depletable natural capital it delivers an output of 44,000 kWh (158GJ) – a 4.4 to 1 return on the original energy investment.

The diesel generator not only requires 5 barrels for its manufacture but a further 60 barrels of fuel to drive it. Its return on the original energy investment is 0.08. Now if one computes *strong sustainability* the economists' way, both appear worthwhile. Here are the figures. Note that since no one can forecast the future price of electricity all calculations are done in what is called 'constant money', a zero inflation concept. This puts the value of the 44,000 kWh delivered over the lifetime of the wind turbine (using current prices for electricity) at £3520.[4] A typical cost for a 1 kW wind turbine is about £1300,[5] and for a diesel-driven generator about half that. Thus the investment of £1300 in the turbine yields £176 worth of electricity per year. To establish the realistic cost of the electricity one has to take account of the potential monetary yield that could be obtained by investing £1300 elsewhere. If we assume this might be 8%, then the cost of the electricity from the wind turbine works out at between 5 and 6 pence per unit. Though this is cheaper than the electricity an individual can buy from the power company, it is much higher than a power company will pay to the owner of a wind turbine. A wind generator passes the test of strong sustainability, but so does a diesel generator, yet it manifestly absorbs more energy than it yields. To truly determine the merits of the diesel-driven generator in monetary units one needs to know the future price of oil (the source of diesel); an unknown factor. At mid-2000 prices 60 barrels of oil refined as diesel (and taxed) cost £1500. But a few months later it cost as much as £2500.

Though both calculations show an advantage to the wind turbines, only the physically-based calculation can tell if the system is truly a sustainable investment.

Why energy is so important

Economists sometimes get very cross with energy analysts for making out that energy is more important than other inputs to the economy.[6] But the fact of the matter is that nothing can be made, transformed, extracted, purified or moved without it. And once used, the capacity of that energy to do anything more is gone for good. Furthermore, unlike all other inputs to the economy, there is *no* substitute for energy. We have no option but to accept nature's immutable laws. Whatever the abundance or otherwise of energy resources, does this not make energy unique? In economic-speak one can extend their abundance by investing in energy conservation. However the laws of thermodynamics place a limit on how far even the cleverest economist can take that argument. Conservation is a one-time gain. There comes a point when there is no more potential for further improvement. The real trouble with energy conservation, though, as a way of extending energy resources is human nature. Let's call it the 'happy hour' effect. When something is cheaper or when we get more for less, we are inclined to indulge ourselves. For example we may heat more rooms in our homes, or maintain them at a higher temperature, or drive our new fuel-efficient cars more often and further. A demonstration of this is that though there have been massive government efforts to encourage energy conservation, with grants and improved building codes, domestic energy use has not declined.

Energy has some of the abstruse and abstract qualities of money. You cannot touch energy any more than you can physically touch your soul or your mind. It is a concept invented by scientists to explain the physical world. What you can feel is heat which is how most of us think of energy, aided and abetted by the advertising campaigns of the energy industries. But the key use of energy is to do physical *work*. Whereas money, as we argued in Chapter 4, measures human work, using the word in its familiar social sense, energy measures *work* in a physical sense. The two forms of measurement together provide most of what has to be known to make an assessment of the viability or sustainability (that is, durability) of a proposed policy or technology. In the rest of this book work in a social sense – which is a process of making decisions, such as those that depress the correct keys in order to type these words – will be distinguished from *work* (in italics) in a scientific sense, which is subject to the laws of thermodynamics.

Energy as work: work as energy

Next time you climb the stairs or a hill remind yourself that you are doing *work* in a scientific sense. The minimum amount of *work* to raise your body up to a certain height is your weight (W) times the height climbed (H) times the gravitational constant (g).[7]

Work = height * weight * g

The speed with which you climb the hill is determined by your power. A frail person can climb to the same height as a strong one, but having diminished power, takes longer. Similarly a car that accelerates from nought to 60 mph in eight seconds, requires a more powerful engine than one that takes 20 seconds, and accordingly uses more fuel. Few people appreciate that the way to achieve fuel economy in a car is not so much by driving slowly as by not accelerating more than absolutely necessary – and this means not braking more than necessary also.

If you were on holiday and were asked by the hotel reception to carry your own suitcase up three flights of stairs, you might consider it an irritating burden but you would not think of it as *work*. However if you were the hotel porter or bellboy you would be working in two senses. First, in the decision-making sense, your job would involve you in making several decisions such as to which suitcase, up which stairs, to which room. Second, in the scientific sense, you would also be doing *work* in expending effort in order to carry up the luggage.

In the natural world there are very few accessible forms of *work*. Falling water can provide *work*, as in a hydro-electric plant. Wind can directly provide *work* through a turbine. Waves carry enormous power, but the means of harnessing them is still at the trial stage. Lightning can provide *work*, but we have yet to learn how to harness this source. Our principal sources of *work* are obtained at one remove using heat sources like oil or coal mediated by engines. Turning this into practice was the seminal contribution of the eighteenth-century engineers Thomas Newcomen and James Watt that propagated the industrial revolution. From that time access to *work* no longer depended on animal or human effort.

Once again nature imposes some rigorous conditions. The amount of *work* you can get out of a given quantity of heat is not fixed. It depends on two things: the difference between the temperature of the heat and the temperature of the surroundings, this difference being expressed as a proportion of the temperature of the heat source (see footnote for the maths[8]). What this means in practice is that heat can never be turned into *work* with 100% efficiency. In fact in the everyday engines of today 35% to 45% is considered as good as it is possible to get. You may have noticed that you get hot climbing a hill because the work you do finishes up as waste heat. An out-of-shape person gets hotter than a physically fit person, who uses body energy more efficiently. Neither can produce *work* at 100% efficiency.

The distinction between heat and *work* is a tricky one to comprehend. For example there is more heat in all the world's oceans than would be produced by combusting all the world's oil deposits. But the oil can produce more *work*. This is because the difference in temperature between the hottest and coldest sea-water is no more than 30 degrees, whereas oil burns at a temperature of several hundred degrees. Thus in practical terms what matters is the temperature of the heat in relation to the surrounding environment. When it is quoted that the theoretical maximum efficiency of a diesel engine is 54%, what is meant is that of the heat that can be obtained by burning the diesel oil, at most only 54% can be converted to *work*.

The human body as a source of work

With the advance of technology we have pretty well given up using human beings as sources of *work*, though there are still peasant communities in the developing world for whom their own toil is the main source. An average human adult can *work* at a rate (power) of 70 watts. So if attached to an appropriate machine, say bicycle pedals linked to an electrical generator, she or he could illuminate a 70 watt electric lamp. Using a human being to do *work* is a poor use of the decision-making skills of even the most ill-educated of us. At the current (year 2001) minimum wage in the UK, one hour's work (as a decision-maker) will buy enough electricity to light almost seven hundred 70-watt bulbs for one hour! It is much more cost effective to employ human beings for decision-making.

The huge material advance of civilisation has been due to the replacement by machines of the limited human and animal potential for *work*. To give some perspective to this, each European citizen is supported, on average, by the equivalent *work* capacity of about 30 energy slaves, beavering away in their interests, day and night. Each North American is supported by 55 such energy slaves. It is true that these slaves do not have to be fed, watered or clothed, but they do absorb non-renewable fuels at a prodigious rate and require machines to mediate the energy.

Here's an experiment to help in understanding the distinction between heat and *work*. You may need some good friends to help you. Imagine that you are in a place with no electricity or other fuel source, and you want a hot bath. Your only resource is your human strength and that of your friends. You fix up a bath tub with 50 litres of water in it and a paddle that can be driven round and round by turning a handle, and you and your friends resolutely take turns at this task. The friction of the paddle will warm the water. Let us suppose it is perfectly insulated so that any heat gained is contained. Let us further assume that you and your friends are averagely fit adults. It would take thirty hours of constant paddling to raise the water to a bathing temperature of 50°C!

Now what has happened here is that the energy you and your friends put out was indeed *work* in a very real sense. It ended up as heat. Supposing you now decide after all to do without the bath, and turn the heat back into *work*. This is where Nature has us over a barrel. At most only 9.3% of the heat produced at 50°C can be turned back into *work* (assuming this was done in a room at, say, 20°C). This is a poor reward for 30 hours of unremitting effort! Furthermore this is the theoretical maximum, and in practice we never can achieve the theoretical maximum, it being a natural law of life that no system (or person) is ever 100% efficient.

Production as a form of work

We tend to think of production as some assembly line operated by skilled workers. They are certainly doing work in the social sense. They will be doing very little *work* in a scientific sense, for that is being done for them by energy mediated by machines. However their social contribution is vital because of the continuous input of decision-making. Take the example of making (say) washing machines. The workers are assembling many parts, mostly made elsewhere in other factories. In scientific terms this can be described as a procedure for reducing chaos (or randomness). These parts are being *organised* by the workers into a single entity: the washing machine. The significance of this is more easily understood by considering the reverse process. Imagine your old washing machine has seen its day, and you give it to a child to play with. He or she will naturally set about dismembering it, eventually to be surrounded by hundreds of parts – screws, bolts, bits of plastic, a pump or two, some insulated electrical wire and so forth. Chaos indeed!

Production is a process of introducing order and reducing chaos.

The science of thermodynamics informs us that whenever randomness or chaos is reduced and order thereby created there is an energy price to be paid. This is known as the '*work*' of transformation. It is possible to compute the required amount from first principles. In real life the actual *work* is always greater than the theoretical minimum. Even in efficient systems it may be twice the minimum.[9] Bear in mind that even the mental process of organisation requires a small, very small, energy requirement. We see this any time we switch on a personal computer.

Thus far from there being any hope of a constant capital rule or *strong sustainability* in the physical sense there is not even the possibility of a zero sum game. As must by now be clear, nature is fair but not entirely benevolent. Scientists express her caprice in the two fundamental laws of thermodynamics. In popular language the first law states that there is no such thing as a free lunch, and the second law that you cannot break even anyway.

Energy as a source of order

The principle source of order in our Earth has been the sun's radiation. Through a process of photosynthesis the chaos of random molecules of carbon dioxide, water and nitrogen in the air become ordered as molecules of plant cellulose and protein. In this way we have trees and crops. Thus over millennia have decaying plants been turned into fossil peat, coal, oil and natural gas. Bronze age Man used cellulose in the form of wood to reduce the disorder of copper-bearing minerals into the more ordered condition known as bronze. Today the human race is so numerous and has such huge material desires, that photosynthetically produced order, such as trees and plants, cannot begin to furnish sufficient energy in adequate quantity to run our economies, and so we have turned to exploiting fossil energy. It is quite irritating to hear certain environmentalists arguing in favour of abandoning oil for biomass. There simply are too many people and not enough land. Our footprint is too large. To quote the biologist David Bellamy, each day we sacrifice 7000 years of photosynthetic accumulation that went to form fossil fuels.

And indeed sacrifice is the right word because once used the usefulness of these energy sources is gone – for ever. Clearly, then, the continuation of economic activity implies the continued availability of energy in the right amount and of the appropriate quality. At worst, like some impoverished banana republic, future generations run the risk of eventually running out of the ability to maintain their physical infrastructure. This was very sharply pointed up in October 2000, when a train crash in England led to a re-assessment of the rail infrastructure. The investment proved so huge that it took several months to complete, and precipitated several bankruptcies. The human race is living on borrowed time. But we do have enough time if we take the right action now. How is discussed in Chapter 10.

Bringing nature into the equation

There's more to nature than minerals, soils, creatures and bio-diversity. nature is a construct of interacting relationships. While human beings can change course randomly and behave irrationally, nature is governed by a set of immutable laws. Scientific study has elucidated many of these. We have a pretty good idea of how most things function, even in biology, and when we do not, it is not because we have got the laws wrong, but because we have yet to disentangle the enormous complexity of the system. For example, the laws that govern the atmosphere and oceans are well defined and proven, but the interaction of ocean and atmosphere is so complex that scientists have yet to be able to predict weather reliably. Anyone who endures the fickle weather of the British Isles can vouchsafe that fact. As for global warming, the complexity is such that a perfectly reasonable case can be put forward that it has nothing to do with our burning of fossil fuels, although the considered opinion differs.

To repeat, it is the availability of energy as *work* that makes it possible to extract ores from the ground and turn them into metals. It is *work* that enables us to manufacture human-made capital, purify the water supply, propel vehicles and aeroplanes, and so forth. Work in the social sense cannot do that. That sort of work is in managing the various processes. A highly placed international functionary known to the authors once angrily dismissed these scientific assertions, saying that the march of technology would eventually make it possible for a Boeing 747 to cross the Atlantic on a litre of fuel. The scientific reality is that it would not even be able to leave the starting block. Science may be irritating, but at this level, at least, it is certain of its ground.

The advent of machines fuelled by energy has meant that the essentials of life support can be produced with a declining proportion of the population, freeing up time for creative and recreational pursuits. It also means that if fuel were to become scarce, life would become harsher.

Economic activity today is a blend of work and *work*. The peasant, driving the ox that pulls the plough, *decides* where to furrow. The ox, dragging the plough, does the *work*. The potential productivity of the ploughman is enhanced with better or more oxen. It is even further enhanced when he or she sits at the controls of a tractor. In this way human physical *work* is diminished, but economic value is enhanced. The ploughing *work* that may be managed by one tractor driver today is about 200 times greater than could be done by a person a thousand years ago.

The reader will have realised that it is not the tractor that actually does the *work*. The tractor is a machine able to take in a refined form of fossil energy, diesel, which upon controlled combustion in the cylinders of the machine does the *work* of pushing down pistons. Through mechanical linkages these drive the wheels of the tractor. Indeed, in an echo from the past, we still talk about machines having such and such a horse-power, the diesel-driven 100 HP tractor being notionally able to do the *work* of 100 horses, which in turn can replace the efforts of six hundred human beings.

Two salient points arise from this simple analysis. The first is that the tractor, as a machine, is useless without fuel. Fuel is the source of the *work* achieved. Secondly, though tractor drivers do indeed have to exert some physical effort, that effort is tiny compared with the output of the tractor. As we have seen, their value is that of decision-makers, even though society may classify them as manual workers.

There is a third and important social point. As long as there are tractors and cheap fuel to power them, the number of people required to plough the land and grow crops will be a small fraction of the population. Thus, though in one sense the combination of technology and fuel has liberated most of the population from the physical effort of providing food, it has also deprived many of livelihoods.

What has just been described is part of a continuous evolution taking place since people first tilled the soil. It is an evolution that is still far from its climax. Already it is possible for a tractor to be remotely controlled; the future farm-worker may be a computer operator!

The same, of course, applies to most manufacturing processes. First, human *work* was replaced by machine *work*, reducing employment (and triggering the Luddite riots in England) but nevertheless expanding the productive potential of the economic system as a whole. Today we are in the midst of the next phase, where decision-making is being taken over by programmed machines. This new situation is not simply an extension of the earlier one. Whereas it takes much energy to produce machines, it takes very little energy to drive the computers and micro-processors that are replacing human decision-making. Expanding production no longer carries with it the automatic potential for increasing employment. Hence the emphasis on services these days. This rupture between output and employment means that for a modern economy the labour supply is no longer a constraint on output, as far as quantity is concerned. It is the educational attainment of the labour supply that is important; that is, its decision-making capability. However the rate of replacement of labour by machines and information technology has now reached the stage where at least three per cent annual economic growth is needed just to maintain the existing labour force in work.

A fourth factor now emerges. The tractor is human-made capital – HMC. It has to be built, assembled from components comprising metals and plastics, etc. Each component is fabricated from materials drawn from nature's store, and transformed into metals, alloys and other derivatives. These transitions all require that *work* be done.

The link between work and money

In chapter 4 we drew upon the work of the American economists Hall, Cleveland and Kaufmann who showed that there is a link between price level, money supply, velocity of circulation and energy. To obtain their impressive correlation between theory and statistical data they had to make some assumptions about the efficiency with which energy was used in the American economy. From the arguments presented earlier in this chapter, is it not clear that it is *work*, not energy, that should be used in their equation? Their 'efficiency of energy use' is best interpreted as the degree to which a unit of heat can be turned into *work*. The fact that not all energy consumed is used to produce work and a fair proportion is used for heating could explain the divergence of their data from their model. So we would propose their equation be modified to:

price level = (money supply * velocity of circulation)/ work used in the economy

The maths behind all this is given in Appendix 2 to this chapter.

Cyberspace

We are in the midst of a communication revolution. The future, we are told, lies in knowledge-based activities. We should not take this to mean we can survive economically simply through superior means of communication. Things still have to be made, food still has to be grown, people will still travel and heat their homes. *Work* in the thermodynamic sense will continue to be needed as much as before if not more so. Even if our groceries, books, or cars can be ordered on the internet, they have first to be produced and then transported. The internet will not curb energy use, it will not make energy use more efficient. It can spread information more widely, but its net effect is to stimulate, not constrain. It may usher in a new way of doing things. That is all.

Now that the distinction has been made between human work and nature's *work,* the next chapter will explore more closely the ways in which different forms of natural capital contribute to that *work* and to our well-being. The crucial question asked is how long can they continue to do so.

Appendix 1: Cost equals decision

Consider the costing of a product as seen through the mind of an accountant. Broadly s/he would see it as the sum of the cost of four classes of inputs:

raw materials	R	cost, £/unit physical output
labour and management	L	cost, £/unit physical output
depreciation of capital	K	cost, £/unit physical output
fuels (energy)	E	cost, £/unit physical output

Expressed in mathematical shorthand cost (C) per unit physical output in any monetary units, L, will be:

$$C = R+L+K+E \qquad \qquad ...1.1$$

To arrive at the price we must add profit, allowing for tax and competition.

Taking any one of the raw materials, one can write a production function in which the cost is some function of labour, capital and energy. In mathematical shorthand:

$$C_R = S_R(R,L,K,E) \qquad \qquad ...1.2$$

And if there is a mix of raw materials, then the same equation holds, only the relative quantities of L, K and E will vary and the coefficient S_R will alter.

Taking capital, and considering it as physical equipment, then we can again use a production function, because physical equipment is simply a particular form of manufactured product. Thus:

$$C_K = S_K(R,L,K,E) \qquad \qquad ...1.3$$

where the K in the right hand equation is the capital used to make the physical capital equipment.

Then, considering fuels (energy), these have to be extracted and purified much as raw materials do, and so we may write:

$$C_E = S_E(R,L,K,E) \qquad \qquad ...1.4$$

where K and E are the capital equipment and energy required to extract and purify the energy and turn it into a marketable fuel.

Remember that each of these equations is in monetary units per unit physical output. These could be tables, chairs, whisky, oil or machine tools. Now if each element in equation 1.1 is substituted by equations 2, 3 or 4 as appropriate (as many times as necessary), all the R, K and E terms disappear, leaving the cost to be the sum of all the labour and management (=human effort) required to produce the many and varied inputs to the goods. These costs can apply to previous times in many places, home and abroad. One gets the same result no matter how many inputs there are, how varied, how old they may be. Cost is the sum of all labour and management (i.e. human costs) over time and space and nothing else:

$$C = (\text{ labour costs (money units)} \qquad \qquad ...1.5$$

Appendix 2: The link between energy (as work) and price

Let Q be the rate of physical output in the economy. Since there are a huge variety of physical outputs we need some common denominator with which to sum them. Let that be the energy (expressed in units of standard quality) irretrievably consumed in making the physical products. Let us enumerate it as the amount of energy embodied in their manufacture. By energy embodied is meant fuels used in actual production, where all types are expressed in terms of a single standard quality. It also includes the energy to turn raw energy into marketable fuels. The implication of this is to equate all types of energy to their *work* potential —

Let P be the exchange value placed upon the sum of all goods, in monetary units per year. Then the average price index, I, is calculated as follows:

price per unit physical output, I = P/Q monetary units per energy embodied   ...2.1

(A convenient energy unit is a billion joules or giga-joule, abbreviated to GJ. One GJ is an amount of heat equivalent to combusting 21.7 litres of oil.)

If the money supply (the amount of money in the economy) in any one year is M, and if M is less than P, then the only way that there can be enough money to buy all the goods is if the money goes around more than once in a year. This is called the income velocity of circulation of money, v. It has the dimensions of 1/time. Normally it is greater than unity (i.e. money goes around the system more than once a year). Nobody has yet come up with a theory to explain how it may be manipulated to achieve particular results, but it is known that it varies with the interest rate. This would seem logical, as when interest is low, people seek credit more readily, and spend more.

Thus the money flowing through the economy per year is M * v and this must equal P,

$$P = M * v£/y \qquad ...2.2$$

and,

$$I = (M * v)/Q £/GJ \qquad ...2.3$$

Money supply is another tricky one. It is not just cash, not just bank current accounts or deposits. It could be stocks and shares and all sorts of financially tradable items. Economists give these quantities various names like M0, M1, M2, etc. The work of Hall et al. (reference 7, Chapter 4) suggests that M2 is the appropriate convention.[10]

If equation 2.3 is valid, then changes in M and v for a given physical output should spell out the inflation rate. This was confirmed by the studies of Hall and co-authors. Their equation may be re-written thus:

$$I = (M * v)/(E * n) \qquad ...2.4$$

where E is the total energy consumption per year, and 'n' an 'apparent energy efficiency' coefficient that is always less than unity. E*n can be replaced with embodied *work* consumed in producing output. A surrogate for *work* can be the actual energy (as heat) if it is expressed in equivalents of standard energy quality. This is the quantity Q. Then equation 2.4 becomes:

$$I = (M * \upsilon)/Q \qquad\qquad ...2.5$$

This is the link between money and the means of production, or put another way, between decision and the means of implementing those decisions.

Notes

1   *The Value of the World's Ecosystem Services and Natural Capital* , R. Costanza et al. 1997, *Nature*, 387, pp 253-260.

2   Energy analysis is a methodology for determining how much primary energy has to be extracted from the earth in order to deliver a product or service to the market place. It was first given prominence through the International Federation of Institutes of Advanced Study at an international workshop in Sweden in 1974.

3   This power rating is about the average annual for a small dwelling in the UK, i.e. using about 24 kilowatt-hours a day, 365 days a year.

4   Also in 'constant money', that is, discounted for inflation.

5   This price is for a single 1kW generator. A wind farm of many generators would reduce the cost by 20 % to 30%.

6   Quoted from an interchange with the head of Cambridge Econometrics, Dr. Terry Barker who wrote to Farel Bradbury, a colleague of the authors: 'As an economist, I do not regard energy as especially different from transport, telecoms or computing power... We could measure output in terms of telephone calls required, just as we can measure it in energy units, but it is a pointless exercise...'

7   Climbing hills on the moon will be easier because the moon being smaller than Earth, its 'g' is less.

8   The efficiency of turning heat into work is given by the Carnot equation. In 1824 the French engineer Sadi Carnot showed that the proportion of heat that can be turned into *work* from any source of heat depends on the difference between the source temperature and the sink temperature. To work this out take the temperature of the heat source, subtract the temperature of the surrounding environment (called the sink), and divide the difference by the temperature of the heat source. Express this fraction as a percentage

9   This is because the theoretical minimum energy requirement is only possible at a zero rate of production, and in real systems, of course, we need a positive rate of production.

10   M2 comprises notes and coins in circulation and private sector current account deposits plus time deposits at deposit banks.

6

Natural capital

If we have available energy, we may maintain life and produce every material requisite necessary. That is why the flow of energy should be the primary concern of economics.
FREDERICK SODDY, NOBEL PRIZE WINNER IN PHYSICS, 1926

Capital is something we accumulate, that can then be invested to yield a return. The playboy who lives off his inherited capital is eventually impoverished. Yet this is just what we are doing with *natural capital*. It is our inheritance, comprising the physical and biological environment, the minerals below the surface of the earth, fresh water, the oceans and atmosphere. Nature is a philanthropist who freely opens her purse to every demand, leaving it to us to choose whether to guard her wealth or dissipate it in self-indulgence. For centuries many cultures, particularly in Asia, saw the environment as something to be managed wisely and to be lived with in symbiosis. Then the great European exodus to America brought with it a culture which regarded nature as a commodity to be owned and exploited. Only very recently has a counter-trend emerged. Nowadays practically the only forms of natural capital not yet subject to ownership by people are the atmosphere and the sun. Even here the urge to command ownership rights is strong. Recently a water company in England sought to charge a householder who was collecting rainwater from his roof! The ocean's fringe has been appropriated to give states territorial rights to exploit marine life and the ocean bed. Taking possession of these rights is like acquiring capital; the Seychellois make a good income from leasing their fishing rights to itinerant Japanese fishermen.

Much as one may deplore the human instinct to possess, there may be a case for ownership of natural capital on a global basis; for according to economic theory unless something is owned and provides rent it is not cared for. Already the atmosphere and oceans are treated as free global sewers. The very vastness of the oceans blinds us to their fragility. The way we use them is a prime example of Hardin's *The Tragedy of the Commons*, mentioned in Chapter 3. It is in all our interests to see that none of our priceless commons are ever over-exploited. We need to become custodians, rather than possessors.

However, natural capital is not simply of one type. Indeed it can be thought of in four distinct categories, the exploitation of which each carries different implications. They will be examined in turn:

- depletable natural capital
- renewable natural capital
- recyclable natural capital
- environmental space.

Depletable natural capital

A stock is not necessarily depleted when used, if its exploitation turns it into something that can later be restored to its original state. The snowflake falling into the river is still a water molecule, and may through the complex processes of the atmospheric cycle become snow again. Water is a recycling asset. The term *depletable natural capital* is used to convey the idea of *once used always gone*, a process of irreversibility, such as when we consume fossil and fissile energy resources. The casual phrase 'energy production' so often used in everyday speech is an oxymoron. Energy can be exploited or transformed, but not made. By incredible good fortune we find ourselves living in a world where the stocks of energy are still huge, but they are nonetheless finite. As Table 6.1 below shows, we are dipping into the store at an astounding rate, driven by the exigencies of population and economic growth. So how much is left to carry humankind through life's journey? When will the store run out? To the first question there is an approximate answer. To the second, none, for it is not yet clear what steps humanity will be prepared take to secure its future. This will be discussed in a later chapter. For the moment let us deal with the question of what remains.

As the years have passed estimates of world energy resources have risen and risen as geologists, usually funded by oil companies, have penetrated further and further into the remote corners of the earth's crust. This has led to a certain complacency, especially on the part of the economics profession whose underlying theory promotes the idea of perpetual price-driven substitution. But, to repeat, there is no substitute for energy.

The consensus is that we now know pretty well what is the ultimate resource base, though one can never be certain how honest companies or governments are with the information they release. Figures supplied may (or may not) include what sceptics refer to as 'political reserves' which are non-existent oil that governments report for their own purposes: inactive reserves (which cannot be extracted with existing technology); and 'frozen' reserves which are suspiciously reported as constant year-on-year.

The best of the latest compilations is that published in 1998 by Nebojsa

Nakicenovic, a prominent researcher at the International Institute for Applied Systems Analysis (IIASA) near Vienna. Energy resources are divided into two classes: *reserves*, which are reckoned as exploitable at present prices, and *resources*, which are known or thought to exist but are not exploitable at present prices with current technology. This second category of energy-in-waiting may be described as '*if you want it badly enough you can probably get it, but it will cost you*'. As we point out later, this cost is best expressed in energy terms, that is in the amount of energy that has to be dissipated in order to bring forth the next unit of energy.

Anyway that which today is classed as a resource will eventually become a reserve, but at a price. But as there exists no paradigm in economic theory with which to forecast energy prices, no-one can say what that monetary cost will be. However if natural capital is measured in *physical* terms, it is possible to factor in the energy lost in the effort to access these less accessible resources.[1]

A recent review by the World Resources Institute[2] in Washington DC supports the IIASA survey, and points to two surprising facts. The first is the degree of consensus amongst a wide variety of expert analysts. The second is that forecasts of estimated ultimately recoverable oil have remained remarkably steady over the last two decades, with an upper estimate of 2400 billion barrels with advanced (but energy-intensive) recovery techniques and a lower estimate of 1800 billion. These figures are larger than the currently known oil resources and reserves, and take account of what is reckoned still to be discovered. According to oil geologist Colin Campbell of Petro-consultants in Geneva since the underlying science is well understood, 'large tracts could now be confidently written off as non-prospective'.

Because the numbers which quantify the world's energy resources are so huge there is real difficulty for those of us who buy our fuels on a day-to-day basis relating to them. If you are an average European you will be consuming energy at a rate of 150 giga-joules of energy each year, but you will probably ask, 'What on earth is a giga-joule?'[3] You may have some idea of what you *spend* on energy, at least directly as car and heating fuel, but not the slightest knowledge of the amount of energy that amount of money represents. Even less will you know the energy embodied in the goods and services you buy.

As far as depletion of resources is concerned, what matters is the physical quantity consumed. The numbers become even less meaningful if you are told that the world's energy stock is about fifty thousand billion (fifty million million) giga-joules. So let us leave such numbers to the experts, and express the world's energy stocks in terms of the percentage that has already been used up and the percentage still remaining. This is the bottom line, as the accountants are wont to say.

Table 6.1: World reserves and resources of fossil fuels as estimated in 1998. The right hand column shows the years of reserves in hand as at 1999 assuming demand continues to rise in a business-as-usual fashion. Source: Nakicenovic.[4]

Energy source	percentage of world resource consumed between 1850 & 1998	percentage remaining	years in hand taking account of probable future consumption
Oil: conventional	37	63	35
unconventional		100	
Natural gas:			
conventional	23	77	60
unconventional		100	?
Coal	21	79	133

On the face of it these global figures support the optimists. Even if things have to change it looks as if there will be plenty of time to fix them. But it is too simplistic to see oil as a vast tank that can be accessed just as easily when it is full as when it is empty. This is not so. As the oil reservoirs are drawn down the effort to extract the rest will be proportionately greater, and that effort will not only be human, but call for expending more and more energy. Also the figures hide huge regional discrepancies. At the moment the European Union can furnish only a quarter of its energy from indigenous sources. The rest has to be imported. By 2015 local supplies will provide less than one fifth. A few countries, notably in the Middle East, have vast reserves, and thus significant financial and political clout. Colin Campbell reckons that by 2009 Middle East states will be providing 50% of the world supply, thus being more or less able to dominate oil prices. The 'desert storm' liberation of Kuwait from Saddam Hussein had, we suspect, more to do with geo-politics than Kuwaiti freedom, just as the Falklands war was not merely about retaining British administration of a distant piece of land. The cost in lives, money and energy in both wars is a measure of how important governments regard ownership of oil resources.

Furthermore it is to be expected that, as the less industrialised countries develop, oil demand will be pushed up. The per capita consumption in India is, at the moment, merely 3% of that of the USA, 7.7% for China; yet the combined population of these two countries is six times that of the USA.

There are just four things that one needs to know about depletable energy resources: how much there is, how long they will last, what sort of pollution they create, and what are the alternatives. The feasibility of these options is closely related to what it takes to extract and refine them. Table 6.1 provides information on the first two points. In considering the other two we shall look at each major energy type in turn.

Oil is an extremely versatile substance comprising many different hydrocarbons. It is liquid, easily stored, and can be fractionated or converted into a huge range of highly useful products varying from petrol and diesel fuels to drive engines, to plastics, lubricants, bitumen, tar and heating fuels. Its versatility and transportability makes it the most valuable of all the fuel resources. On combustion, between 3.1 and 3.9 kg of carbon dioxide are formed per kilogram of oil, depending on the length of the carbon chain in the molecule. Thus the pressure is on environmentally to use low carbon hydrocarbons, like natural gas which contains only one carbon atom coupled to four hydrogen ones. LPG (liquified petroleum gas) produces 4.6% less carbon dioxide than petrol for the same amount of heat.

Liquid fuels can be made from other sources but this is technically complex and consumes a lot of energy in the by-going, thus making the carbon dioxide output even larger. The South Africans have for years converted coal into liquid fuels, as did the Germans during the second world war.

Natural gas is twice as abundant as oil. It is mostly distributed by pipe-line, tanker or bottle. For the moment it is the world's cheapest fuel. It burns cleanly and produces about a third less carbon dioxide per unit of heat than liquid fuels. Thus it is every government's choice as a way of meeting its Kyoto protocol commitments without actually cutting back on energy use. It can also be a precursor in the manufacture of plastics.

Old king **coal** is still abundant, but has three disadvantages. It is labour-intensive to mine, it is dirty and it produces more carbon dioxide per unit of heat than even liquid fuels. With natural gas freely flowing through the pipeline networks that cover three quarters of the world, coal has gone out of favour. But eventually coal will be needed. Here there is a real problem. Will it ever be possible to resuscitate the skills and culture associated with underground mining that made it such an intensely comradely activity in spite of its dangers? China is the world's biggest producer and consumer. It was once wryly said by the chairman of the Club of Rome that the best way to reduce greenhouse gas emissions would be to give China one free nuclear reactor a year!

There are other sources of hydrocarbon even less accessible than coal: tar sands and oil shales. These need to be roasted in ovens to drive off the oil. This is an exceptionally energy intensive and polluting process.

Finally there are **fissile** fuels, such as uranium and thorium, that can be used in nuclear reactors. Here the heat of nuclear fission is converted into steam, which then drives a steam turbine to generate electricity. These minerals are very thinly distributed around the earth's crust but abundant enough, especially if the by-product of fission (plutonium) is used in another sort of device known as a fast reactor[5] which is able to breed nuclear fuel.

Remember that the key role of energy is to do *work*, without which nothing can be produced. Heat is often a luxury, *work* is essential.

Care must be taken in interpreting Table 6.1. It refers to energy resources in the ground, and has not taken into account the fact that energy has to be spent to extract energy. Supposing geologists told the oil company boss that in such and such a location there lay a potential billion barrels of oil. The petroleum engineers would then be asked to work out what it would take to extract this oil. Let us say that, taking account of the energy required to build the oil rigs, pipelines etc. and then to pump out the oil and refine it, the equivalent of a quarter of a billion barrels is needed. This means that the *net energy* yield would be three-quarters of a billion barrels. So to all intents and purposes the reserve is not 1 billion barrels but three quarters of that. In technical language one would say that the net energy was 0.75. The net energy obtained from oil shales and tar sands is much poorer than for oil or gas but there too the trend is worsening. At the moment, between the *work* of extraction, transport and refining about 7-10% of the oil taken from the ground is dissipated. Thus the numbers in Table 6.1 do not really represent the potential energy available for actual use in our economies.

Today the world is almost entirely run on depletable natural capital, particularly oil and natural gas, and is becoming more dependent on it with each passing day. For something so central to our way of life, the very driving force of the economy, it has been astonishing to note the indifference, or is it the incomprehension, of the economics profession. Even after the member countries of OPEC[6] managed to quadruple the price of oil (first in 1974, then in 1978) the message was still not getting through to the a-physical world of the economist. The following example is taken from a paper delivered at the height (1978) of the OPEC-induced crisis by two well respected resource economists.[7]

> While it is plain that the characteristics of an optimal depletion policy depend crucially on whether or not a resource is essential, it is not *a priori* plain as to what constitutes essentiality!!

The exclamation marks are ours. Energy, that is depletable natural capital, *is* the one essential resource. If we cannot secure a sustainable supply we are done for. Given a supply of this vital ingredient, almost any of our other physical requirements can be met, be they fresh water, obscure elements, or synthetic fertilisers. In their seminal paper 'The Age of Substitutability' Arnold Weinberg and Hans Goeller of the Institute for Energy Analysis in Tennessee expressed themselves bluntly.

Our technical message is clear: dwindling mineral resources in the aggregate, with the exception of reduced carbon and hydrogen (i.e. oil and gas), are largely a myth. But the exception is critically important; Man *must* develop an alternative energy source.[8] (Original emphasis)

If we are to approach the future in a rational manner, we must invest some of what's left to secure a future sustainable, that is durable, supply from renewable sources. To do less would be grossly unfair to future generations. Necessity may be the mother of invention, but here action must be taken before necessity becomes obvious.

Recyclable natural capital

When bronze-age man made vessels and tools of bronze, you can bet that they were never thrown away when they had outlived their usefulness. Those that weren't buried with the dead to help them on their celestial journey were recycled – melted down and re-formed into something new. Bronze was bronze and remained so, endlessly recycled.

Indeed every physical thing we use, whether we eventually discard it or not, is still physically on the planet. Potentially everything is recyclable. In other words there is no absolute loss of physical materials. Consider a resource like iron ore. Even after it has been extracted and smelted into iron, then used to make a product such as a car, there is just as much iron in the world as there was when it lay in the ground as an ore. This is still true when the car's life is ended, and it becomes scrap. That iron is never destroyed but remains within our physical system, and is therefore theoretically always accessible even if it has become dispersed. There are always just the same number of iron molecules in the world, and their properties are unchanged. The same may be said for gold or any other physical material that is extracted, refined and used.

The idea that we may be depleting the world's non-energy physical resources is a false one. Like gold in the ground to gold in the vaults of our banks, they are merely being transferred from one locus to another. Nothing is lost. Naturally the richest lodes are accessed first, because extracting these require the least energy *work*, but as time passes we have to move on to leaner ores. Here is the snag, as may be seen from Table 6.2 which records the consequences of depletion in the case of copper ores. Note two points: first, there is a huge increase in waste associated with exploiting leaner ore bodies. This means that mining will become more unsightly and polluting. Second, an enormous increase in energy is required. A US Academy of Sciences report noted:

... the problem is to avoid reaching a point when exploiting those mineral deposits which remain will be too costly, because of depth, size or grade, so that we cannot produce what we need without completely disrupting our social and economic structure.[9]

When *Limits to Growth* [10] was published in 1972, it depicted a world economy eventually crashing from a deficit of resources. In frustration the economist Beckerman[11] countered by reasoning that there could be no shortage of physical resources for the obvious reason that just in the top one kilometre of the Earth's crust lie enough ores, even as basic rock, to last the world '100,000 years'. Actually he is insufficiently optimistic, since the top one kilometre of the earth's crust represents some 432,000 trillion tonnes of rock, enough for some 800 million years at present rates of use! As to sheer quantity, one cannot dispute his argument.

Table 6.2: The environmental and resource implications of extraction and refining: now and in the future. Source Kellog.[12]

	today rich ores	post-2000 lean ores	distant future basic rock
Ore grade: % copper	0.7 %	0.2%	0.01%
Tonnes waste rock per tonne copper metal produced	355	940	6,300
Tonnes tailings per tonne copper metal produced	145	620	12,500
Total waste: tailings + waste per tonne copper metal	500	1,560	18,800
Energy required per tonne copper metal in GJ	97	275	5000
% increase in energy required compared to 0.7%	–	280%	5100%

Another economist, Banks,[13] points out that if one assumes three per cent world annual economic growth, the 100,000 years becomes 500. Quite so, but then the 800 million years becomes four million years. So on this score nothing seems terribly pressing.

In fact neither of these statements is particularly illuminating, for both omit the critical factor, illustrated in Table 6.2. It is the increasing energy needed to extract and refine minerals. The bottom of Beckerman's 'top kilometre' is one kilometre down. Deep mines are costly. Oceans cover a great proportion. As extraction moves to leaner ores or less accessible places the effort in capital and energy to access them grows ever larger. It is reckoned that over the next 25 years there will have to be a 50% increase in world annual capital investment for resource extraction and refining, much of which is due to the shift to leaner ores.[14] Even so, this will be less than 10% of the world's annual capital investment.

So in one sense physical resources are just about infinitely abundant; not, however, if we are talking about their economic availability. It is worthy of note that 66%, by weight, of all material extracted from the earth is fossil energy, whereas its abundance in the earth's crust is a mere 0.004%.

Whether or how we recycle our discards is a human choice. It may be made on economic, or resource grounds, and sometimes nowadays on environmental principles. The disposal of the Shell oil company's 'Brent spar' oil platform is a rare case where the environmental lobby won, thanks to Greenpeace. In fact the poor of this world are the best exponents of recycling. One does not see plastic bags abandoned in Nepal (except by tourists) or cars junked at 6 years old in Cuba.

All that is needed for recycling is ingenuity, human-made capital and fuels. It is this last item that tends to get overlooked. Fuel was at the centre of the famous milk bottle debate of the mid-seventies. The question posed was: 'is it less energy intensive to recycle glass milk bottles than to use discardable cartons?' The answer centred on how often the bottles could be used before they got broken. These days we are everywhere enjoined to place our discarded bottles in bottle banks, and all our milk comes in cartons! Bottles are largely made from silica, one of the world's most abundant ores, so the practice of recycling them has nothing to do with a scarcity of silica deposits. However it has everything to do with reducing energy consumption and avoiding mountains of discarded bottles.

Renewable natural capital

Strictly speaking there can be no such thing as renewable energy, because no energy source is renewable. We earthlings can use the term only because the earth receives a huge flux of energy from the sun, and the sun is sufficiently durable for us to ignore its eventual demise aeons from now. This wonderful, wonderful sun is a nuclear fusion reactor situated a safe 150 million kilometres distant. It beams energy down upon the world at a rate that is ten thousand times greater than the present world fossil energy demand. In other words, in one single day the solar radiation impinging on the earth is equal to 30 years of world energy consumption at 2000 rates. Problem over? Not quite. Though technologically we know how to harness the sun's radiation, it has a habit of disappearing at night. More significantly, capturing the sun's energy tends to require a lot of human-made capital.

There are other forms of energy which are recurrent: tides and the geothermal heat oozing out from the earth's molten core. Here we confine ourselves to outlining the essentials. To evaluate a renewable energy system five pieces of information are necessary, and we shall explain why. They are the capital (as HMC) needed to build the devices; their likely lifetimes, their load factors (we'll come to that); the area of land required; and the quality of the energy they produce. Let's take the this last aspect first.

The point has already been made that the most important quality of an energy source is its ability to do *work*. Though anything that generates heat can produce *work* if that heat is mediated through an appropriate engine, as we saw in Chapter 5, the proportion one can extract is dependent on the temperature of the heat source compared to the surroundings. In practical terms, electricity is the most potent form of *work* available to the market. At the other end of the scale, passing down through natural gas to oil and coal, is wood-fuel. The ability of biomass to do *work* is about one sixth of that of electricity. So by and large in the western world we do not use it for such purposes but for the homely warmth of a wood stove with its agreeable reek. Biomass (or bio-energy as it is often called) can never be more than a minor contributor to our energy needs because we simply do not have enough spare land to grow it.

There are a number of renewable energy technologies which directly produce electricity such as wind turbines, photo-voltaic cells and wave energy devices. The first requires wind, the second strong daylight and the third ocean waves. The trouble with the first two is that the wind does not always blow, nor the sun always shine. Moreover the wind may be a zephyr or a gale, the sun is often obscured by cloud, and winter days are shorter than summer. The upshot of all this is that renewable energy devices are rather like a car, which stands idle much of the time, yet the capital cost is the same whether it is used or not. The fraction of time these devices are fully employed is called the *load factor*. Depending on the wind regime or the sunniness of the climate, typical load factors are in the region of 15-20%.[15] This is why they have difficulty competing with traditional fossil-fuelled sources of energy at present energy prices. Any factory working only 20% of the time would be out-competed in no time. Moreover these devices are not at all cheap. In fact, per unit power, photo-voltaic devices are at the moment more expensive than nuclear reactors, and wind turbines only a little less so. The renewable energy devices seem cheaper because they can be built in small units (e.g. 1 to 300 kilowatts), whereas the smallest nuclear reactor has a power output of about 600 thousand kilowatts.

The lifetime of these renewable energy devices is much the same as for conventional electricity generators, about 20-30 years for wind turbines, and more for photo-voltaics. No one yet knows for sure about wave energy. Not enough wave turbines have yet been built.

The combination of capital cost and low load factor means there is more capital tied up per unit of actual energy delivered, a point already made in Chapter 5 in the example of the wind turbine. Table 6.3 compares the output per unit investment of wind turbines and photo-voltaic arrays calibrated against the most capital-efficient device of the present day, namely the so-called combined gas turbine (CCGT) that burns natural gas.

Table 6.3: Output per unit investment of various electricity generators compared to gas-fired (combined cycle gas turbine) generators, which have the lowest investment cost of any current system.

Technology of generation	Load factor	Output per unit investment CCGT = 100
Gas-fired combined cycle gas turbine (CCGT)	typically 80%	100
Nuclear: pressured water reactor	typically 70%	50
Coal-fired	typically 80%	90
Wind-power	23% (windy regime)	30
Photo-voltaic	6% (cloudy climate)	15

Renewables, however, can vastly reduce pollution. The Energy Technology Support Unit (a UK government research station) estimates that an installed capacity of 50MW (i.e. about 1/1000 of UK installed electrical generating capacity) would reduce carbon dioxide output by 594 thousand tonnes, sulphur dioxide by 3711 tonnes and nitrogen oxides by 1884 tonnes (all annually). Using polycrystaline silicon cells, this capacity would require a surface area of cells of 4166 hectares, about the area of ten large farms, or the roof area of about 10,000 houses.

Renewable energy sources have an uphill economic struggle. They have to compete against coal and gas. However a recent study argues that if the environmental costs of pollution from coal, oil or gas-fired electricity are taken into account (i.e. internalised) the true price of electricity would be higher, and thus render renewables more competitive.[17]

Hydro-energy

The least capital-intensive way to garner renewable energy is from the kinetic energy of falling water. The trick is to drop the water down a pipe from as great a height as possible. This usually requires the building of a dam. Hydro-systems already provide about 17% of the world's electricity and do so without producing any carbon dioxide or radioactive wastes. Of course it means flooding valleys, often ones that are fertile and occupied by farmers. Naturally they resent this. The huge projects planned in India and China require the relocation of millions of people, and involve heart-breaking losses for those who have been born and bred on the expropriated land. The Himalayas represent a huge untapped potential, though the risks from earthquakes will probably limit expansion.

Storing renewable energy

The great advantage of fossil-energy sources is that they lie in large stores underground, ready to be withdrawn as needed. Renewable energies are for the most part transient. Storing heat on a small scale is possible, but cumbersome. Storing electricity in a battery may solve a domestic problem for a while, but will hardly keep the wheels of industry and commerce turning.[18] The one successful solution is to use spare electricity on good days (from a renewable energy point of view) to pump water uphill to a dam, so that on the poor days, power can be re-generated as it flows down, as in a hydro-power station. This is called pumped storage. It is easiest where the terrain is mountainous. In flat countries where there are deep caverns underground, a surface lake can be to a cavern what an upland dam can be to a river below. There is a small loss of power in such systems, but then nothing associated with energy is ever a free lunch.

The fourth aspect of natural capital, environmental space, is a big topic calling for a chapter all on its own.

Notes

1   There is a maxim that one must spend money to get money. The same applies to energy. One must spend energy to extract or harness energy. This is known as the 'Energy Requirement for Energy' – ERE, and may be determined from a knowledge of the physical location, concentration and type of the energy source.

2   See World Resources Institute at www.wri.org/wri/climate/finitoil/euroil.html

3   The unit used in many energy-economic analyses is the giga-joule (GJ). Giga is the scientific shorthand for a billion – a thousand million. Thus a GJ seems like a lot of energy, but this is not so because the joule itself is a very small unit of energy, but of an internationally defined and accepted standard. It takes about 2 million joules (of fuel converted into electricity) to bring a domestic electric kettle full of water to the boil, so 1 giga-joule (GJ) could service five hundred kettles. As petrol it could propel a thirty-mile-per-gallon car 180 miles.

4   *Global Energy Perspectives,* N. Nakicenovic, A. Gruber and A. McDonald, 1998,

Cambridge University Press. Their Table 4.4 is a compilation from many other sources such as the International Energy Agency, the World Energy Council and the US Geological Survey.

5   Most nuclear reactors work on the principle of slowing down the neutrons that are emitted on nuclear fission. Plutonium-fuelled reactors use high-speed neutrons which can be captured by non-fissile and abundant Uranium 238 and so converted to Plutonium, thus breeding its own fuel. Such devices are inherently more difficult to control than conventional nuclear reactors.

6   OPEC – Oil Producing and Exporting Countries, consisting of Middle East, African, Asian and South American countries, with the HQ in Vienna. It is committed to maintaining the price of oil by restricting the output of the member countries.

7   Pariah Dasgupta (London School of Economics) and Geoffrey Heal (University of Cambridge).

8   *The Age of Substitutability*, A. Weinberg and H. Goller, 1976, *Science* 191: pp177-178.

9   D. Frasche, 1963, 'Paper 1000-CJ' of the National Academy of Sciences committee on natural resources, Washington, DC.

10   *Limits to Growth* , D. Meadows et al., 1972, Universe Books, New York and in many other countries. This was a path-breaking study, but because it treated *all* resources as depletable, it failed to highlight the key role of energy.

11   *Economists, Scientists and Environmental Catastrophe,* W. Beckerman, 1972, Oxford Economic Papers.

12   H. Kellog, 1973, quoted in P. A. Bailey, *Mining Engineering*, January 1976, no. 34.

13   *Natural Resource Availability,* F. Banks, 1977, *Resources Journal*, March.

14   The model used here is known as GlobEcco. It was developed for the museums department of the French Ministry of Research in 1992 as an interactive display for visitors. Though it has not been updated to the latest data, the basic elements of the model are unchanged, and the model has tracked the evolution of the world since 1992 adequately.

15   Much more efficient arrays are used in space modules. A 32% efficiency of conversion of solar energy to electricity has been obtained with certain 'multi-junction' cells, but their cost is many times higher.

16   Report ETSU/a/p2/00240/rep, ETSU, Harwell, UK.

17   These are costs covered by society at large. A major EU-funded study spanning ten years and with many institutions co-operating examined conventional electricity generation using the methodology of *impact pathway*. It concluded that between two and eight cents (US) should be added to

obtain the real costs to society of producing electricity from conventional sources. Nuclear-generated electricity came out of the study rather better. EXTERNE project.

18   A step forward has been made in using a regenerative fuel cell. Spare electricity makes hydrogen, which is later reconverted to electricity. This allows storage on a much larger scale at a cost of about £120 per kWh stored, a reasonable price.

7

Living with nature

The nation that destroys its soil, destroys itself.
FRANKLIN D. ROOSEVELT

Nature is dynamic. She destroys as well as creates. The ecologist Holling[1] calls it creative destruction. Australian aborigines, the supreme masters of survival, deliberately fired their lands to bring rebirth to the seeds. We humans are co-actors in this process of change. However being the dominant species means that we shall, as it were, still destroy the last dodo if our own immediate survival is at stake – whatever our professed convictions. Our practical responsibility is to prevent that situation ever arising.

There is plenty of historical evidence that human activity can destabilise an ecosystem when too much is demanded from it for too long; witness Mesopotamia in the first millennium of the Christian era or the collapse of the Easter Island community. The Roman Empire's excessive demands caused the decline of output from the North African grain basket. It is the very same greed that destroyed the Newfoundland cod fishing, and a similar fate is facing the fishermen in Britain. The difference between the survival of a fish stock and its disappearance is so fine as to be unpredictable. And when the fish disappear communities suffer. So we move from an ecological disaster to an economic and social one.

The resilience of a system lies in its ability to withstand the knocks of random events. With a non-resilient (brittle) system a quite small disturbance can topple it. More than likely the underlying reasons for a collapse have been long-present but unnoticed. This is why the phenomenon of global warming is so worrying. Slight rises in sea temperature may be enough to disturb that great Atlantic conveyor, the Gulf Stream that warms northern Europe. Were it to be disturbed Europe might experience a new ice age.

Resilience is not only an ecological concept. Economic systems are at their most vulnerable and brittle when they are at the peak of their efficiency. As the old adage has it, 'the best is the enemy of the good'. A recent example is when at one and the same time the Channel tunnel was out of commission and the French truck drivers blockaded the ports. Those manufacturing enterprises which had adopted the latest efficiency idea of just-in-time deliveries of parts were forced to interrupt production.

Management for resilience may well require us to adopt a lower rather than higher pitch of labour efficiency. And in attempting to contain the greenhouse effect we shall in all probability have to be satisfied with less energy-intensive life-styles.

To implement a strategy for resilience three conditions must be met.

The first is that it be agreed at international level *not* to pour into the air, water and earth more wastes than these sinks can assimilate. Here we are talking about environmental space. So far, as we have seen at Kyoto in 1997 and Bonn in 2001, it has not proved easy to obtain that agreement; but at least governments are trying. One problem is that while what we emit can easily be quantified,[2] it takes considerable science to determine what the limiting capacity is – especially when scientists are also charged with assessing what will be the cumulative effect of these wastes through years to come. No one forecast the hole in the ozone layer, or that the migration of CFC (chloro-fluoro-carbon) gases through to the stratosphere would have such a strong effect. The case for increased investment in environmental research is unassailable. For the moment we must manage on the basis of uncertainty.

The second condition is that strong sustainability (as discussed in Chapter 5) be achieved in the physical sense, not merely in the economic sense. That means evaluating human-to-nature interactions in physical terms. Management for resilience cannot be drawn up in financial terms.

The third condition is that the eco-system (of which we are a part) be viewed as a set of feedbacks. Linear management, where a decision invokes an action without taking account of how the outcome affects subsequent events, is a recipe for disaster. A method is necessary for determining *in advance* what would be the overall effect of a given action; and this cannot be left to intuition, informed guess, or some extension of past trends into the future. The process starts with an analysis of the structure of the whole system, identifying mechanisms, feedbacks, linkages and time lags. Quantified physical systems analysis is vital.

None of this will be easy in a world where competitiveness is considered the path to progress and where the criterion of success is profit and financial dominance. Nor is the situation helped by the role of the World Trade Organisation; a point further developed in Chapter 11.

Waste

Everything we consume, from fish fingers and bread to consumer goods and nickel-cadmium batteries, finishes up as waste in one form or another. In the developed world about ten tonnes of waste are produced for each tonne of useful goods. One person's waste is everyone else's burden.

The environmental space needed to handle waste varies enormously. To adequately dilute the effect of chloro-bi-phenyls, cadmium or alpha emitters requires a huge amount of space, or special decontamination measures. Coal ash, by contrast, is relatively innocuous. Absolute quantities alone do not tell all.

One of the wonders of modern urban living is that our wastes are magically taken away. Apart from having to pay for the service, their disposal is no longer a matter for our personal concern so long as it is not dumped in our own back yard; somewhere else, if you please. Of course, in principle, we are all environmentalists. In practice most of us are merely notional adherents. A small minority are truly responsible. Judge yourself by responding to the following: Does your lifestyle reduce the world's stock of non-renewable resources? Do you, or does someone on your behalf, discard your wastes into the environment? If you answer 'no' to either of these questions, you are either a magician or living like a Kalahari bushman. The fact is that if you have income and spend it you are, however indirectly, dissipating non-renewable energy and laying claim to environmental space.

That's why, even if the reader is all for a better environment, as opinion polls show most of us are, there are practical difficulties in the way if you want at the same time to lead a modern existence.

So is the whole environmental bandwagon a chimera? In one sense, yes it is. But we can try to tailor our economic activities to the capacity of the environment to handle them. A truly environmental approach would be to organise our society on the principle that there is no such thing as waste as such, only another potential resource. The trouble is that not everything can be recycled. Some wastes inevitably need to be stored, like certain nuclear fission products. But the real catch-22 is that recycling almost inevitably requires the expenditure of energy, which creates its own waste. One can think of very few exceptions; composting of garden waste is one. Unfortunately it generates greenhouse gases!

The hole-in-the-ground approach to waste disposal has had its day. Few things arouse a community's ire more than a proposal for a nearby rubbish tip. And all holes eventually get filled up. No one complains about a sewage works that quietly disposes of toilet waste as a weak stream of organic fluids. But even a sewage works has a limit to its capacity. The critical factor here is population density. Indeed if it is low enough industrial treatment is not even necessary. Many a rural dwelling relies on a septic tank. At a further extreme reflect on the three Inuit families who spend their summers on the south shore of Scoresby Sund, a huge Greenland fjord at latitude 70° north. There they hunt seals and walrus. They enjoy no sewage system or rubbish collection. Their wastes just accumulate as a rotting sludge outside the only door of their summer shacks. But do they worry? Not at all. Each winter the action of snow, frost and foxes restores everything to a pristine environment (apart from tin cans); moreover without any human effort, energy input or capital investment!

Three hundred years ago in Edinburgh's famous High Street with its tall enduring tenements, the occupants were not so favoured. They threw their garbage out of the window giving, by custom, a cry of 'Gardy-loo'[3] to warn those walking below. Towns were known in those days for their unpleasant odours and unsanitary conditions although rain from time to time washed the mess away.

Environmental space

The Inuit hunters place no stress on their environment, for on the whole of the 1800 miles of the East Greenland coast there are barely 2000 inhabitants. Their environmental space is huge in relation to the wastes they generate. Not so for modern cities. Edinburgh graduated from its 'gardy-loo' mentality to dumping its wastes at sea, maintaining cultural continuity by naming the sludge vessel *Gardy-loo*. But even this method of waste disposal is no longer permitted as the North Sea has insufficient capacity to moderate the now huge volume of waste generated by all the contiguous countries.

Aubrey Meyer of the Global Commons Institute offers a useful analogy. He asks us to imagine a tap running into a bath, and flowing out of the plug hole at the same rate. The bath's volume is environmental space; the water flow a surrogate for pollution. What has happened, however, is that some kinds of pollution have blocked the outflow so that the water now overflows. The essence of the problem is that the Earth has a finite land area and biosphere into which to fit a growing world population. With six billion inhabitants[4] and 149 million square kilometres of land we are down to an average of only two and a half hectares of land space for each one of us on earth and it is getting less by the second. If the median UN population projection of 9.3 billion by 2050 should turn out to be correct, then we would be down to one and a half hectares each – which would have both to absorb our wastes and provide our food. Already in China each hectare of arable land supports eleven people on a simple diet. As living standards rise that one hectare will no longer satisfy their needs. Even in agriculturally favoured areas like Europe certain high population density regions like England and the Netherlands must import food, if only to support livestock production.

The Nobel prize winner George Borgstrom aptly described land that produces these imports as the *ghost acres* of these countries.[5]

Our understanding of atmospheric and ocean dispersion is still uncertain. A particular ocean, taken as a whole, may be large enough to dilute a pollutant but will it disperse evenly? To assume so is to imply that there is a giant teaspoon at work. In fact the processes of bio-accumulation are well documented; pollutants become concentrated first in simple organisms and then even more so in the predators that eat these organisms. The concentration of the pollutant thus increases as it moves up the food chain with humanity having the unfortunate privilege of sitting at the top. It is quite possible to be poisoned by someone else's quite innocent (or legally permitted) use of environmental space.

The Italian futurist Cesare Marchetti has proposed an audacious 'dilute and disperse' method for carbon dioxide, which he describes as a *gigamixer*. His idea is to pump the gaseous emissions from fossil-fuelled furnaces into thermohaline (sinking) ocean currents, at points where they start to dive deeply, such as at the Straits of Gibraltar, the Red Sea, the Weddell Sea in the Antarctic, and the North Atlantic. Because of the slow rate of mixing of these waters the gas may reside in the deep oceans for thousands of years, being released slowly over time.

Such a scheme does, however, face a number of major uncertainties such as the effects of the gas on deep water ecology and the actual absorption capacities of the deep oceans. It might well upset the feedback loops that lead to atmospheric oxygen concentration being stabilised, discussed earlier under the Gaia hypothesis. And so one problem is traded for another. When we ran Marchetti's idea through our global model we found that the electricity demand for pumping the carbon dioxide into the oceans was so high that it led to a significant rise in electricity demand, which if fossil-fuelled would significantly increase the amount of carbon dioxide to be treated! It was like running to escape your shadow.

What it takes to put it right

We have to start by understanding production. Every system has at least two outputs – a useful product and a waste stream. The product, too, will eventually become waste when it is worn out and discarded. There are also at least two physical inputs: physical capital structures (the HMC mentioned in Chapter 5) and energy. The HMC will eventually wear out as well and be abandoned, while the dissipated energy is an immediate source of pollution in forms such as carbon dioxide, nitrogen oxides or radioactive wastes. It is hard to think of any economic action that does not finally end as waste[6] even if recycled. If, as an individual consumer, you want to embark on a one person crusade to reduce waste, there is no better way than to live on a reduced income.

Even the infrastructure becomes waste in due course. Though some structures have lasted for centuries, such as the arena at Verona, the Red Fort near Delhi or the Mayan temples in Guatemala, they are the exceptions. The colossus of Rhodes, the hanging gardens of Babylon or the lighthouse at Alexandria have all perished. On a more mundane level your car, dishwasher, shoes, even your house are all destined to become waste. The trick, if it can be found, is to make use of the waste. Thus are cow pats turned into a nitrogen-rich manure. But what can be done with a dilute stream of chemicals leaving a papermill? One of the ironies of the computer age is that far from creating the paperless office, more paper than ever is being used.

However progress is being made. Many cities now burn their waste, though paradoxically this also consumes fossil energy to foster the combustion. Engaging market forces can also work well through the concept of trading pollution rights. This has been very successful in reducing sulphur dioxide emissions. If one country or region is not using its full allowance, then it may sell these rights to other some region or industry that cannot yet control its emissions. We extend the idea to energy in Chapter 9 with a proposal for Personal Energy Rights.

Measuring the impact

If you believe at all in equity then it follows that we must share the global environmental commons. At the moment the western industrialised countries are absorbing a disproportionate share. At least so it is averred. Let's look at some numbers. Two obvious impact indicators are population density and economic output – GDP. That these are but partial measures of pressure on the environmental space may be seen from the sample in Table 7.1.

Table 7.1: Two popular criteria of environmental impact: a sample of eight countries

Country	population density: people per km^2	population per hectare arable land	economic impact: GDP per capita (Bangladesh=1)	net food importer or exporter
Bangladesh	750	12	1	importer
Netherlands	400	16	85	importer
England	350	12	80	importer
Israel	220	14	52	importer
France	110	3	94	exporter
Kenya	50	13	1.7	importer
Saudi Arabia	7	12	30	importer
Iceland	2.5	31	131	importer

Ask yourself which country has more impact on the environment? Populous but poor Bangladesh or the rich but less populous Netherlands? Both need to import food and therefore use ghost acres. Netherlands citizens are eighty-five times richer using the conventional criterion of GDP; and whatever caveats one may have about GDP as a measure of welfare it *is* a measure of activity, and therefore of a tendency to generate wastes.

People live on land, and the area available per capita represents part of the potential waste-absorbing capacity of a country. So while GDP per capita may be a reasonable measure of impact in one sense, it needs the land term to provide an insight into the pressure on environmental space. For this reason GDP per unit area is a more revealing measure. However linking energy use per unit of output to area offers an even more sensitive indicator. These two impact measures are compared in Table 7.2.

Table 7.2: A comparison of GDP per unit land area, energy use per capita and energy use per unit land area as possible measures of impact on environmental space. Selected countries are enumerated as proportions of world average: GDP/km2=US $ 850,000; Energy per capita = 66GJ; Energy per km2 = 2737 GJ.

Country	GDP/km^2	energy use/capita	energy use/km^2
World	100	100	100
USA	6700	400	260
Netherlands	7500	300	2000
England	6100	220	1800
Switzerland	5600	160	600
China	5.8	50	150
Costa Rica	10.5	100	150
India	8	120	80
Mexico	10	70	80
Brazil	6	30	14
Kenya	1.5	15	5
Nepal	2	10	3

Any well travelled person would find that energy use per unit area conforms closely to one's impressions on the ground. Such a measure does, however, upset some well established preconceptions. For example the USA which is chastised for emitting 25% of the world's carbon dioxide while having only 5% of the population, actually puts less pressure on the environment than most European developed economies because of its large area, and hence low average population density. The booby prize goes to the Netherlands followed closely by England and Belgium (not shown in the table). China, though often damned for poor environmental management, has such a large area in relation to its energy use that (for the moment) it sits in a median position. Brazil similarly has still much room for manoeuvre. Both countries are developing fast and will soon be beyond the critical intensity.

This indicator of energy use per unit area is also one adopted by the Canadian ecologist William Rees.[7] He has put forward the charming concept of the ecological footprint. This he describes as an area of land large enough to absorb a country's human-made wastes while also yielding enough food, water and raw materials on a sustainable (that is, durable) basis. He expresses the ecological footprint as so many hectares required per capita, and for Canada he calculates it to be 4.7 hectares. His colleague Mathis Wackernagel later revised the figure upwards[8] to 7.4 hectares per person. The area of Canada is 9.22 million square kilometres and the population is 29 million, so there are 340 hectares available per person. One might conclude, then, that Canada's ecological footprint is well below its population carrying capacity. However, much of the land is mountainous, arctic tundra, glaciated or barren. The true ecologically productive land is much, much less. Wackernagel estimates that this reduces the *available* capacity from 340 to 12.6 hectares per person. However that is still well above the footprint. On such reasoning there would appear to be ample scope for Canada to expand its population and industry and to increase its material standard of living without exceeding the threshold environmental space. It is one of the few countries in the world in such a good position.

A different picture emerges if the same calculation is made for an urban region such as Vancouver. Rees calculates that it has a footprint nineteen times greater than its actual urban area. This shows clearly that the idea of a 'sustainable city' is absurd. A city is only sustainable by virtue of its hinterland.

An even greater disparity between *available* capacity and *actual* footprint is to be seen when one looks at the figures for the more intensively populated regions of the world. Rees' calculation of the footprint for the UK is 2.65 hectares per capita, whereas he estimates the ecologically productive land to be 0.35 hectares per capita, a huge deficit! Wackernagel more recently updated the figures to 4.9 and 1.8 respectively. Our ECCO model assesses the UK's ecological footprint at 3.05 hectares per capita, some fifteen times the *available* capacity.

The footprint is a wonderful way of highlighting the dual nature of environmental and resource pressure resulting from human numbers and their material standard of living. There is scarcely a developed country whose footprint does not exceed its *available* capacity. The approach has the merit of transparency, but inevitably it is imprecise. There are simply too many value judgements to be made in arriving at the numbers. Moreover it is a snapshot of the past. For a dynamic assessemnt of the future footprint one can use a natural capital accounting model of the economy.

Research into measuring the impact of waste on the environment is at a very early stage. Literally hundreds of indicators have been put forward[9] dealing with specific aspects. No one indicator can capture the total effect. Moreover indicators serve only to give us snapshots of the past, whereas what we need is to get a grip on where our habits are leading us; to find a way of assessing the holistic impact of our activities and of the environmental space needed to cope with them. In short we need to generate what is called an 'environmental cost function'. Only it need not be in monetary units; it could be in energy terms. Here is an example.

Burning sulphur-containing fossil fuels produces a pungent gas called sulphur dioxide, which in strength can kill, but at a distance is merely unpleasant. Once in the atmosphere it reacts with oxygen and water to become an acid, and then falls as acid rain. It does our forests and shrubs no good. So very rightly the European Union has set targets for reducing sulphur dioxide emissions. There are four options:

- Using only low sulphur fuels.
- Removing the sulphur from the fuels.
- Taking the sulphur dioxide out of the flue gases.
- Not burning fuels at all, but investing in renewable energy systems.

The first option is limited by the lack of low sulphur fuels. The second option is very expensive, and cannot easily be used for coal. The third option, however, is technologically feasible, as is the fourth.

David Crane[10] examined these options using the ECCO natural capital accounting model of the United Kingdom to generate an *environmental cost function*. He set out to explore whether the technical fix of removing sulphur dioxide from stack gases when using sulphur-bearing fuels was better or worse than generating the required electricity from wind turbines (no fuel use). The criterion of 'better' that he took was the gain or loss of national economic output resulting from each option. His analysis showed that on the basis of this criterion it was much more effective to use the technical fix of flue-gas removal. However the renewable energy option, using wind turbines, dispenses with not only sulphur dioxide but also carbon dioxide. If one took that into account as well, the balance of advantage shifted to the wind turbines.

A way forward

There are many people who believe the solution to reducing environmental impact is to revert to a simpler life-style; a new Erewhon. Unfortunately at current population densities this option alone is insufficient. Moreover in the developing world people are anxious not only to achieve decent standards of living, but to enjoy the fruits of the market economy and the stimulus it gives to creative endeavour. Time magazine, for one, is certain that new technology can 'heal the environment, not harm it'. While this is undoubtedly true of certain technologies, it is untrue of many others. Some propositions are simply not thought through. Let us look at three proposals that at first sight seem to offer real solutions but turn out to have thorns on the rose.

- **Bio-diesel**. This seems like a great idea. Grow your own tractor fuel! Certain plants such as rape-seed produce an oil which can substitute for diesel fuel. It is sulphur free and has been claimed to produce one quarter of the carbon dioxide of conventional diesel per unit produced. That last claim, for one, is not true. More seriously, there is simply not enough land to produce anything more than a tiny percentage of the diesel demanded. Furthermore, if output is raised by treating the rape fields with fertiliser then logic demands that account be taken of the energy used to make the fertiliser in order to assess the net energy yield of the overall system. Put simply, bio-diesel can only be viable where arable land is in surplus. Is there such a place?

- **Fuel-cells**. How to do away with fossil fuels! A fuel cell is a device which transforms certain fuels such as methyl alcohol or hydrogen directly into electricity. Fitted to vehicles they provide a virtually noise free, pollution free (except for carbon dioxide in the case of methyl alcohol) engine. This is a technology with a great future and many of us will have fuel-cell powered cars by the end of the next decade. But, and it is an important but, neither methyl alcohol nor hydrogen are found in nature. They have to be made by using other primary fuels, or from electricity generated by renewable energy systems. If the sources are fossil or fissile fuels, then no energy resource problems are solved at all, though there is the advantage that pollution is centralised where it can be better handled.

- **De-materialisation**. Scientists and economists at the Wuppertal Institute for Climate and Energy in Germany believe that the de-materialisation[11] of production is the way forward to a greener economy. What is needed, they argue, is that production and economic life should be rationalised to use less in the way of material inputs; for example lighter building construction or sharing one's grass mower with a neighbour. They point to how the transistor replaced the thermionic radio valve and greatly reduced material and energy use. Similar innovation, they argue, will cut down on freight, resource requirements and energy and will thereby reduce the demand on environmental space.

It may cut down on the first two. We cannot be so certain about the third – energy.

The idea was endorsed by a group of well-known individuals who met at Carnoules, France in October 1994. Their Carnoules declaration states 'that the productivity of energy and materials is the key'[12] to achieving enhanced human welfare and reduced pollution. It contends that 'a ten-fold increase in resource productivity may occur almost painlessly in many countries'. It is for this reason that the group call themselves the 'Factor 10 Club'.

A move towards dematerialisation is undoubtedly to be supported, but a factor of ten is fantasy, credible only to the technologically illiterate. Naturally it has great political appeal. The *Wall Street Journal* and the *Financial Times* gave the idea a great write-up. It left the business world believing it could sit back; the danger had passed. Three of the Carnoules group expressed themselves more modestly in a book called Faktor Vier (Factor 4).[13] It was a bestseller in Germany. Regrettably, however, nothing we have studied supports optimism even on that reduced scale. But even if it did, there is human nature to contend with. As in the 'happy hour', two drinks for the price of one simply result in one drinking more.

The rebound effect

Another name for the 'happy hour effect' is what the economists call the 'rebound effect'. In a chapter called 'Limits to efficiency', two American authors,[14] Gary Gardener and Payola Sampat, list a number of cases of material reduction, such as diminishing the weight of cars (through a switch to plastics), using bottles instead of cans for drinks (they can be recycled), and recycling lead acid batteries, radial tyres and mobile phones. Significantly they also point out that in each case production has soared. Savings in material reduction have simply led to a greater potential for investment so that the net effect has been more output, and yet more material usage.

Waste management

Since we now have to manage waste disposal, there is a new business endeavour: *w*aste management. It may be recycling, it may be integration of processes, or it may be harnessing the feedback of the market economy to such purposes through legislation. This is serious business and offers huge opportunities. Worldwatch quotes[15] the current chairman of the Ford Motor Company in the USA as saying, 'Smart companies will get ahead of the (environmental) wave. Those that don't will get wiped out'.

The intelligent free-market solution is to regard pollution as a commodity, and issue each country or factory with limited pollution rights. If your own country or factory can cut back on pollution to the extent that you enjoy spare rights, then you can sell them to someone else. Thus while several European countries are hard put to meet their carbon dioxide emission targets Russia, as a result of its economic meltdown, can ease their situation as well as her own by selling her spare emission rights. Such trades buy time but offer no permanent solutions.

Stuffing waste into a hole in the ground also has a strictly limited potential, as we have already remarked, and always raises the question of 'will it stay there?'

Waste is an attitude of mind. In many poor countries an old tyre becomes ten new sandals. The ideal industrial system would absorb every waste as a recycle. We do try, and are trying harder. Paper, aluminium cans and bottles are extensively recycled, perhaps as much as 20%. A satisfying case is that of the technology of scrubbing sulphur-bearing stack gases with a slurry of limestone that has first been reduced to calcium oxide. This produces an innocent compound known as gypsum which is made into those interior wall-boards widely used in building. With due care and attention to location, technology and opportunities, many processes could be rendered much more innocuous.

But there are dangers in recycling as we see in the use of animal carcasses to serve as cattle feed, which led directly to the BSE crisis, or the feeding of restaurant swill to feed pigs. It was this practice in the UK which is thought to have initiated the 2001 foot and mouth epidemic.

Integrating the input and output sides of an economic activity offers most promise where wastes are organic, and therefore capable of chemical conversion. Over one billion tonnes of such wastes are produced annually in the world,[16] including bagasse, animal dung, cereal straw, cotton and papyrus. Though they can be burned to produce heat, it is a poor way to use them. More profitably they can be biologically transformed into a variety of products such as alcohol, methane or furfural (to mention a few), all of which can be precursors to more complex and valuable chemicals. At the moment synthesis from fossil fuels renders these methods uneconomic by comparison, but should there be a tax on energy (see Chapter 9) their economic worth would rise.

Restraint

And so finally to the ultimate solution: personal and corporate restraint. So much of the flow of wastes is market-driven, particularly in packaging. In a typical basket of super-market goods packaging comprises as much as 4% by weight and more by volume. Little of this is needed for product protection. The drain on fossil fuel and forests by today's packaging industry is quite frightening – and internet buying is set to seriously increase the amount of packaging used.

Restraint, though, is not good for commerce. That is the dilemma. This chapter, coupled to Chapter 6, brings home the message that we have to organise our economies to get more out of less, but bearing in mind all the time that the laws of thermodynamics place limits on us. Even recycling has its limits because it incurs yet more capital and energy use. It is the treadmill of a positive feedback loop: a situation exacerbated by the growing complexity of modern society and safety legislation. Governments need urgently to evaluate what are the upper (or outer) limits of national environmental space, and legislate accordingly on the basis of a holistic appraisal. But this takes us right back to another dilemma pointed out in Chapter 1: that politicians are inevitably obliged to ride two horses at once. The prospect of taking the environment seriously creates enormous headaches for them. It means facing the possibility that unbridled economic growth may not be an option.

So how on earth are we to manage the global commons? This is the burden of the next chapter.

Notes

1   'Simplifying the Complex', C. S. Holling, 1994, in *Futures*, 26, 6 pp. 598-609.

2   Natural Capital Accounting is an excellent method for doing this.

3   Adapting the French 'Gardez l'eau'.

4   The six billion mark is said to have occurred on or about 12 October, 1999.

5   *Too Many,* G. Borgstrom, 1967, Macmillan, New York.

6   Some wastes can yield energy if appropriately treated. They may then be said to have 'embedded' energy.

7   *Our Ecological Footprint* , W. Rees and M. Wackernagel, 1996, New Society Publishers, Canada.

8   These figures are higher than quoted earlier and are given in a global study funded by a Swiss bank – see *Ecological footprints of nations: How much Nature do they use? How much Nature do they have?* Commissioned by the Earth Council for the Rio +5 Forum. Distributed by the International Council for Local Environmental Initiatives, Toronto, 1997.

9   An excellent outline of the economic approach is given in *In Search of Indicators of Sustainable Development*, Eds. Onno Kuik and Harmen Verbruggen, 1991, Kluwer Academic, Netherlands.

10   *Balancing pollutant emissions and economic growth in a physically conservative worl,* D.C. Crane, 1996, *Ecological Economics*, 16, pp 257-268.

11   Nothing to do with the delightful antics of the heroes of *Star Trek* who can be beamed up to their space crafts.

12   *Carnoules Declaration*, Wuppertal Institute for Climate and Energy,

Wuppertal, Germany.

13 *Faktor Vier*, E. Von Weizsacher, A. Lovins and H. Lovins, 1995, Droemersche Verlag, Munich. Later English language edition published by Earthscan, London.

14 *Mind Over Matter,* G. Garner and P. Sampat, 1998, Worldwatch Paper 144, p29, Washington DC.

15 Worldwatch 1999 annual, p18, Washington D.C.

16 *Biological Energy Resources,* C. Lewis and M. Slesser, 1979, p37, Spon, London.

8

Sharing the global commons

Whoever said the world's getting smaller never had to fuel it.
ADVERTISEMENT BY EXXON/MOBIL
(JANUARY, 2000, WWW.EXXON.MOBIL.COM)

As individuals none of us can be completely free. At the margin we are bound by social conventions and legal constraints. Nor can countries be entirely free. Hegel said, freedom is the recognition of necessity. Since the world environmental space is finite, we have no moral choice but to share it. In Chapter 3 we dwelt on the essay by the American biologist Garret Hardin entitled *The Tragedy of the Commons*. Recall that Hardin pointed out that where a resource was accessible to all it only needed one selfish individual hogging more than his or her share for the carrying capacity to be over-strained. This would then prejudice the interests of everyone including, in the long run, the individual in question.

Managing the sharing of a commons is not unusual in pastoral communities. In the Scottish Highlands, for example, it is known by the word *souming*. This is an agreement amongst those who share a common grazing to limit it to so many animals per acre, according to the carrying capacity of the terrain. This is affected by climate, soil and solar radiation. It might be decided, for example, that each crofter's (farmer's) share should be eight cattle, twenty sheep and their followers. Each year the crofters meet to decide what is the appropriate grazing intensity, and so fix the *souming*. They may also decide what might be done to raise or lower it, having in mind the need to sustain the productivity of the land.

Extending this approach to global environmental space, upon what basis might a *souming* be defined? Whatever the basis proposed it will be hotly disputed because some countries will surely lose out, and others will gain. It will be Kyoto and Bonn all over again. But a start must be made, and that calls for proposals.

At first glance the size of a national population might seem to offer a logical and fair basis; the more the population the more the environmental space they would have a right to command. One consequence of such a proposal would be that since space is finite, any one country's enlarging population would be at the expense of all others. A further consequence is that it would set in train a damaging feedback since it would encourage population growth. We have seen this in the European Union in the farm animal sector where subsidies to less favoured agricultural areas have been based on animal populations, thus encouraging farmers to intensify animal grazing and produce more animals than the market can absorb.

Mindful of this drawback, Richard Douthwaite[1] has proposed a *souming* based on a population P_c fixed in a base year for all time.

Thus if ES_w is the available world environmental space expressed in km^2 and P_w the population of the world at the base year, then according to him the *souming* would be:

ES_w / P_w km^2/capita

and the total environmental space available to that country would be:

$(ES_w / P_w) * P_c$ km^2

Under this arrangement a country gains nothing by having a growth in population for P_c is fixed. Indeed it loses. This seems unfair to the less developed countries, many of whom are struggling to get to grips with high birth rates. For this reason we suggest another approach later in this chapter.

If, as may well turn out to be the case, global environmental capacity is found to be less than we currently assume – as is believed to be the case with carbon dioxide (q.v. Kyoto, 1997) – then two issues will arise. Firstly the developed industrialised countries will find themselves in deficit, and so will argue tooth and nail against the idea. Secondly Douthwaite's proposal, though an improvement, would be unfair to those countries with high fertility rates because, however intense their family planning efforts, their populations will inevitably continue to grow for many decades. They would be asked to cede part of their future potential.

Another basis could be GDP per capita? Here the *souming* would be:

ES_w / GDP_w km^2/$ GDP

The trouble here is that it would have to work in an inverse way; that is to say that the lower the GDP, the more pollution a country could legitimately put out. This also engages quite the wrong feedback.

What is needed is an allocation principle which is not only based on the environment's capacity to absorb wastes, but which discourages the inefficient use of her depletable natural capital. The seed of an idea was planted in Chapter 7, where it was demonstrated that energy use per unit area was a good macro-economic measure of environmental impact. Why not make this the criterion for a global *souming*? In other words, a given upper intensity of fossil or fissile energy use per unit area of the world's land surface? In this case the *souming* would be:

E_w / L_w GJ energy use/km^2

where L_w is global land area and E_w is maximum non-renewable energy consumption consistent with not over-taxing the world's environmental space. A country's environmental space demand is then defined as E_c/L_c and if this is less than E_w/L_w it is free to expand its use of energy or to trade these rights with another country whose E_c/L_c exceeds its *souming*. In this way the industrialised countries would have time in which to modify their practices and bring on-stream renewable energy sources, while the developing countries would benefit from their ability to sell their surplus rights to them in the form of tradable permits.

To obtain some impression of the impact of such a proposal see Table 8.1, which is an extended version of Table 7.3. Today the world average fossil and fissile energy use is approximately 2740 GJ per km^2 of land area per year (or 65 tonnes of oil equivalent). Suppose for the sake of discussion this be the desired world *souming*, E_w/L_w.

Table 8.1: Energy use per unit area as a measure of pressure on environmental space. Data refers to 1995. Number in last column rounded off.

	Energy use, billion GJ/y	Land area, '000 km^2	Energy GJ/km^2.y	Position relative to world average
World	400	146,000	2,740	1
USA	66	9166	7,200	2.6
Netherlands	3.0	54	56,000	20
Australia	3.1	7617	400	0.14
England & Wales	7.8	160	49,200	18
Switzerland	0.7	40	17,500	6.4
Costa Rica	0.18	51	3,500	1.2
Mexico	4.2	1908	2,200	0.8
Jordan	0.12	88	1,300	0.5
China	34	9326	3,600	1.3
Brazil	3.2	8456	370	0.14
India	6.8	2973	2,300	0.84
Kenya	0.08	566	150	0.05
Nepal	0.013	137	95	0.03

This proposal is not as radical as it would seem. It is already happening in respect of carbon dioxide and sulphur dioxide emissions. However by using energy in a general way, it covers much more than greenhouse gases. This idea first saw the light of day in 1972 at an annual meeting of the UK Conservation Society. The suggested procedure is that on the scientific evidence available, the UN Environmental Programme (UNEP) determines the global *souming*. A World Energy Council monitors the use of energy in all countries and issues an annual statement of how near or far that country is from the legitimate *souming*. Such an organisation would need the power to exert some sanctions, like that empowered to the World Trade Organisation. As we shall argue later, the WTO is in fact the ideal organisation for the job. It merely needs a change of remit.

The proposal has the merit of engaging several important feedback loops. It discourages population expansion. It encourages the development of renewable energy systems. It provides a very real and tangible way for the less favoured nations of this world to sell some of their rights in the short term, thus using a free market mechanism to transfer buying power from the wealthy nations to the poorer.

If, for example, UNEP were to decide that the current E_w/L_w should be the appropriate upper limit, then it may be seen that six of the countries listed are over the threshold and seven are under. And there are some surprises. Australia is in a very favourable situation. All the European countries would exceed the *souming*. The USA, even given its vast area, is also too intensive. Even China in her present state of development and with her vast acres is above the threshold. These countries are occupying ghost acres for both energy and environmental space in much the same way as George Borgstrom's[2] ghost acres for food.

Here are two examples of how the mechanism would work. Supposing Kenya wanted to capitalise on its very low E_c/L_c which from Table 8.1 is seen to 0.05 (or 5%) of the world average, E_w/L_w: (65 tonnes of oil equivalent (TOE) per km^2). Kenya has a land area of 582,000 km^2. Under its chartered right to a *souming* of 65 TOE it is entitled to consume 566,000 * 65 tonnes of oil equivalent = 37 million tonnes per year. It actually consumes only 5% of that. It therefore has a spare right of 35 million tonnes. The value of that right to industrialised countries who have exceeded their *souming* will be of the order of several hundred million US dollars. Kenya is then in the position of not only gaining a useful flow of funds, but funds to which there is no interest payment attached, and which will continue year on year, though diminishing as her economy develops.

Now take the example of the Netherlands whose E_c/L_c is 20 times the *souming*. In other words her consumption of 30 billion GJ (717 million TOE) has to be cut, or the rights to it purchased on the world market through tradable permits. The cost of those rights might well be of the order of US$2 billion a year, or 6% of her GDP.

However other options are open to countries whose energy use per unit area exceeds the *souming*. They can reduce their energy use by efficiency measures or belt tightening, and they can invest heavily in renewables. In the meantime tradable permits provide an interim solution. It will be many decades before many the developing countries, especially in Africa, approach their *souming*.

Though we cannot yet know what the global *souming* would or should be, to judge by the figures agreed at the 1997 inter-governmental Kyoto meeting it will probably be less than 2740 GJ per km² per year. As in the setting of fishing quotas, there is likely to be considerable bargaining and dispute over scientific evidence. It will take time to hammer things out. The important first step is to agree to the principle.

Figure 8.2 re-arranges Table 8.1 in order of use of global environmental space (energy use per square kilometre).

Figure 8.2: Countries in order of their use of environmental space in 1995 compared to world average *souming* (2740 GJ/km²=1).

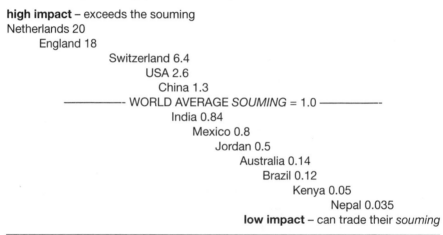

high impact – exceeds the souming
Netherlands 20
        England 18
                    Switzerland 6.4
                        USA 2.6
                        China 1.3
            ―――――― WORLD AVERAGE *SOUMING* = 1.0 ――――--
                        India 0.84
                            Mexico 0.8
                            Jordan 0.5
                                Australia 0.14
                                Brazil 0.12
                                    Kenya 0.05
                                        Nepal 0.035
                            low impact – can trade their *souming*

Globalisation and the souming

How will the principle of the *souming* mesh with the increasing globalisation of trade and production? Will it interfere with consumer choice, a cherished freedom of the neo-liberal economists? Will it put people out of work? Will it be considered just one restriction too many on the now widely accepted principle that wealth is created by giving entrepreneurs a free run?

Indeed it will almost certainly be so construed – but then, as we have pointed out several times, the idea of an ever-expanding economy is a nonsense anyway. The foot is going to have to be lifted from the accelerator sooner or later either to minimise pollution or because fossil energy will have become increasingly scarce. When the authors ran their global model to the end of the current millennium under a business-as-usual scenario, they found that per capita output peaked around 2030. The reason is simply that global population rises to the point where the demands for capital (HMC) to support basic needs exceed the world's ability to produce it *and* expand the economy. This conclusion, of course, takes account of the moral principle that people cannot be left to starve, that they should have shelter and clean water, and that basic services should be sustained. A more cynical view may be that the richer countries will ignore the needs of their less fortunate neighbours. That would surely be the outcome predicted by Ian Angell and Thomas Friedman (cf. Chapter 4).

It takes little imagination to envisage the awful consequences of overall global decline if no preparations have been made for it. Even the industrialised countries would suffer, more particularly as a result of their high levels of national and personal borrowing. Pension funds, endowment assurances and sinking funds would all shrink, and those who depend on them would be made destitute. Mortgages would be foreclosed. The depression of the 1920s took fifteen years and a war to resolve. This new depression might be unresolvable. A wise citizen will make sure that his or her debts have been paid off before the century is too far advanced. Even as we write this a major UK endowment insurance company has had to cut its pension provision in the light of lower stock market yields.

Tempering growth with reason

Application of the *souming* principle would temper growth, but in a way more consistent with the resource and environmental implications of economic expansion. It would provide the world with a softer landing. It would also provide a negative feedback to population growth. In the less developed countries not only does a growing population mean that the available amenities have to be spread more thinly, it also reduces the amount of *souming* that can be beneficially traded. Fortunately there are now very few places left where reduced family size is not recognised as desirable, and increasingly practised. At least here one step along the road to a more durable development is being made.

The *souming* principle may serve to counteract another weakness of the free market economy, namely its tendency to build surplus production capacity. This is the direct and inevitable consequence of competition. For example, today the world's factories can produce 78 million cars a year, though the demand is for 58 million. There would still be enough cars available to meet demand even if the entire European car production ceased. We are in an age of over-production, over-consumption and over-work.

Mail services are another example of over-provision. Fifty years ago when a letter or package addressed to anywhere in the world was put in the post, the arrangements of the international postal union saw to it that it arrived without extra charge. But the new philosophy is to create competition in the delivery of mail. Nowadays there exist some thirty global courier services, and many times more local ones. The result is a huge redundant capacity, involving unnecessary capitalisation and energy dissipation as hundreds of half-full delivery vehicles criss-cross the land, air and sea. Nor is it cheaper. Whereas it costs in Europe about half a euro to send a 20g package (equal to 4 sheets of A4) from one end of the European Union to another by post with a 90% certainty of delivery within 24 hours, a courier service may charge sixty times more in order to deliver it with 99% certainty. More haste but also more energy.

The ease with which money can be created was partly responsible for the Asian financial crisis of 1997-8. With the cold war ended the resulting peace dividend meant that huge amounts of capital were then looking for a home that would yield an aggressive return on investment. As a result of the trade deals effected by the newly formed World Trade Organisation manufactured goods could be exported without restriction to Europe and America. So where better to invest than in the cheap labour of the highly competent economies of Asia? The growth was meteoric. Just prior to the moment of crisis capital stock in certain Asian countries was increasing by as much as 20% per annum, much of it in buildings that now stand empty. Since no investor is armed with perfect information, an excess of productive capacity resulted. With such growth and such competition, the only way European and American companies could compete was by shedding labour or by moving to Asia, just as that pillar of British retailing Marks and Spencer found themselves having to do. The bubble was bound to burst, for there was no underlying physical rationale to these investments.

Another trigger of the crisis was the advice of the International Monetary Fund (IMF) and the World Bank to these Asian countries. Mindful of 1982, when foreign investors lost a lot of money as the Mexican peso crashed, they were told what to do: privatise national institutions, cut taxes, adopt export strategies: but most significant of all, peg the currency to the dollar, so investors would not have to worry about devaluation.

Who could resist investing under these conditions? Whatever happened, a foreign investor's money would be safe. The situation encouraged borrowing and a vast amount of debt ensued, exceeding the national GNP in some cases. There the interest to service these debts rose to a third of the GNP. Meanwhile the local rich had borrowed local currencies, turned them into dollars, and then used them, safe in the knowledge that no devaluation could affect *them*. Never mind the creditors.

Any assessment of the situation using a physical approach would have demonstrated to the World Bank and the IMF the folly of this approach. Had the *souming* been in place a very different investment approach would have occurred.

We have argued in this book that not by money alone will we cure the world's ills. The s*ouming* principle provides a solid base for decision-making, and moves decision-making away from the fiction of money to the hard reality of physical resources and environmental space.

The World Trade Organisation

There can be no international entity that has had such a baleful effect on the global commons as the World Trade Organisation (WTO). It stands like a lighthouse sending out a false signal and so diverting countries into an unsafe harbour. In its present form it will not be happy with the principle of the *souming*, although it should be. For here is an approach that could actually achieve one of the WTO's ostensible goals: helping the developing nations. The WTO has had a bad press, and rightly so. It places in the hands of the transnational companies (TNCs) an unbelievable hegemony over the rest of the world. It does so in the name of trade, and under the argument that the expansion of trade is good for everyone. There is no doubt, to use Korten's phrase, that globalisation has been 'a landmark triumph for corporate libertarianism'. Today, of the one hundred largest economic organisations, fifty-two are corporations and forty-eight are nation states. These TNCs can exploit international disparities in wages and other costs as they please. The more comprehensive the liberalisation of trade, the less they are bound by local or national rules. Not least, trade union and environmental interests can be played against each other or checkmated. In a review of the WTO's first ministerial conference in Singapore in 1996 the commentator Rainer Falk reported that 'the negotiations reflect the dominance of the North's agenda. After the International Monetary Fund and the World Bank, the WTO is the most important pillar in the institutional triumvirate of the neo-liberal world order'.[3]

Launched in April 1994, the WTO's mandate is to eliminate the barriers to the movement of goods, services and capital. The idea is that the rules should be transparent, and from the point of view of commerce, predictable. It is supranational. Article XVI states: 'Each member [state] shall ensure the conformity of its laws, regulations and administrative procedures as provided in the annexed agreements'.[4] Once these have been ratified by a signatory state, that country can no longer control the entry of foreign capital. It cannot favour its own industries or contractors. It cannot ban the import of foreign goods. If it tries to do so, say because it disapproves of the imports (as in the case of genetically modified cereals opposed by the European Union), the exporting country can appeal to the WTO whose unelected panel of 'experts' will pronounce judgement. The burden of proof lies with the defending country. The only defence considered to be valid is scientific. The possible destruction of local industries is not a matter to be taken into account. In other words WTO rules take precedence over the rules and social conscience of individual sovereign states.

Bananas provide a recent example. The European Union, mindful of its responsibilities to former colonies, gave preferential access to these banana producers. American banana exporters, who own huge swathes of territory in Central America, used the WTO in 1999 to oppose this support. They persuaded the US government to slap 100% tariffs on a wide range of European exports from cashmere garments to Roquefort cheese and greeting cards. The EU stood its ground. The matter went to WTO arbitration, and the USA was awarded the right to impose £190 million worth of tariffs per year. In future the EU cannot discriminate in favour of its old colonies. The trouble with winning the rat race is that you are still a rat.

Under the rules, the recommendation of the review panel is automatically adopted sixty days after decision unless there is a unanimous vote of the signatory country representatives to overturn the judgement. This renders the appeal process virtually meaningless.

So why have 136 states signed up for this licence to kill? In the case of the developing countries it was the expectation that WTO would focus on their problems, but in fact the agenda has always been driven by the richer countries. To its surprise, even the European Union has difficulty in resisting American hegemony. The smaller states dare not stay out since they would risk being shut out of world trade by having tariffs set against their exports. A Hobson's choice, it seems. The arguments are, of course, well rehearsed. It is all good for global economic growth. More growth equals more trade equals more prosperity. But there is precious little equality in these equations. They might be acceptable if all people shared in the economic benefits arising. But we are in a free market economy, where there are no soft landings for the less competitive.

The report of the WTO Committee on Trade and Environment was so lacking in substance that at their 1998 Singapore meeting the environmental organisations attending it withdrew. But things move on. In March 1999 the director-general of the WTO, Renato Ruggiero, convened a conference on trade and environment. In his opening statement he said: 'With the WTO we are poised to create something truly revolutionary – a universal trading system bringing together developed, developing and less-developed countries under one set of international rules, with a binding dispute settlement mechanism. I would suggest that we need a similar multilateral rules-based system for the environment – a World Environmental Organisation to also be the institutional and legal counterpart of the WTO. This should be the main message from this meeting'.

This is rather like the owner of a distillery proposing a commission on alcohol abuse. Well, even those who like to drink deplore drunkenness. Can there be a partnership between trade and environment that can respond to the same rules?

There can be, but first there will have to be a recognition that the world is physically constrained. We must make the best we can of the options open to us. To begin with, an enormous amount of trade is irrelevent to people's welfare and unwittingly absorbs resources that could be better used elsewhere in the economy. What is the point of Europe and the Far East trading cars when these days one car is much like another? The *souming* principle fits in rather well with the WTO stated objectives. It might just turn a suspect organisation into something we could all appreciate. We turn to this in the last chapter.

Notes

1 *The Ecology of Money,* R. Douthwaite, Schumacher Society briefing no.4, Green Books, Dartington.
2 Refer to Footnote 5 in Chapter 7.
3 *Development and Co-operation,* R. Falk, March 1997, pp 4-5, Deutsche Stiftung für Internationale Entwicklung, Berlin.
4 The entire text may be seen on the World Trade Organisation's website: http://www/wto/org

9

Redirecting the forces of greed

Taxes should tell the truth.
ERNST VON WEIZSACHER

Anyone who studies the economy in resource terms is naturally drawn to the idea of replacing taxes on income with taxes on energy. Resources are finite, people are not. Income tax is a tax on labour, a tax on people's time. This follows from the discussion in Chapter 4. Time at work is largely spent in management, that is, in thinking and directing. Surely the less we tax our ability to process logical thought the better. Though it may not be obvious value-added tax is also a 'labour' tax. Value is added by people. Does it not seem counter-productive to tax labour, given that unemployment is a major social problem? Why tax that which is abundant and surplus when the other key input to the economy, energy, is finite, dwindling and polluting?

There are three general rules about taxation. The first is that no business pays tax. It collects tax on behalf of the taxing authority. Essentially it is a cost added to the product price. The second rule is that taxation is a money recycling system. The third rule is that the rich are best placed to avoid tax, since they can employ the necessary expertise.

The idea of taxing energy rather than labour fits in well with the requirements for managing a durable global economy. That is: evaluation of all policy objectives through the filter of physical and environmental analysis as well as economic; containment of the forces of corporate globalisation; and a more equitable sharing of the world's depletable energy resources. The global *souming* presented in the previous chapter will assist in meeting the second and third of these conditions. However the focus on the physical obliges us to put energy at the centre of our thinking about development, and at the same time to rid ourselves of labour-based taxes.

There is nothing wrong with taxes. 'Taxes are the dues that we pay for the privileges of membership in an organised society', said Franklin Roosevelt. If intelligently thought out they carry a strong social message. In European countries these dues are high, between 40% and 46% of income.[1] In the USA the proportion of income taken in taxes is lower, but then the social wage is also less. By the time an American family has paid for the services a European gets automatically from the state, there's not much in it.

Where the American is spoilt, however, is in the price of motor fuels which at the time of writing has just risen to about two dollars a US gallon; that is, about 40 pence or €0.66 per litre. The Americans are howling with pain, but that's a price low enough to make a European motorist want to emigrate! The difference is entirely due to tax, the price of oil itself being essentially a world price for one and all. If American energy use was brought down even to European levels, the resulting huge reduction in oil consumption would, through the interaction of supply and demand, sharply reduce the crude oil price. But would this truly be beneficial? Would it not result in a concomitant rise in demand in countries outside the USA? In other words might we not be back where we started, with just as much global consumption of fossil fuels and greenhouse gas emissions?

It should be noted that where governments tax fuels they almost always choose land-based transport fuels. International air and sea transport enjoy tax-free fuels. In many countries this privilege is extended to farmers and fishermen. In other words they are subsidised by the other sectors of the economy. Singling out the private car and the haulier (trucker) seems a little unfair. If energy is to be taxed, then all sectors of the economy should contribute. Anything else leads to the sort of distortion we have seen in pelagic fishing where because of tax-free fuel a fishing vessel can travel enormous distances in search of ever more scarce fish. This is counter-productive. A study[2] of the energy use in fishing off the coasts of Scotland from 1930 to 1970 showed a steady rise in energy use per unit fish caught due to depletion of stocks. But during the 1939-1945 war, fishing declined due to the demands for vessels and men for the war effort. Fish stocks recovered. When fishing re-commenced the energy use per fish caught was back at the level of the 1930s. But not for long as competition encouraged the development of more aggressive methods which were more energy-intensive. By 1950 the energy use per fish landed was twice that of 1939. Now, in 2001, fishing communities all over the world are facing the end of fishing, a fate that has already befallen Nova Scotia.

The very idea of taxing energy draws an instantaneous hostile reaction not dissimilar to that when heroin is withheld from an addict. It is an apt analogy. We are hooked on energy. And on those occasions when motor fuels ran dry as during the 1978 OPEC embargo and more recently in Europe in August and September 2000 (as a result of blockades by hauliers), we behaved like junkies, willing to pay any price for our fix.

If, for whatever reason, some countries in future find themselves obliged to reduce their energy consumption, some mechanism will be needed to constrain the energy-using habits of the people. Rationing is one way but it is a blunt instrument. It calls for much bureaucracy and does not cope well with the widely differing needs of commerce, manufacturing and domestic life. Nevertheless constraint implies control, and successful control, as we discussed in Chapter 3, requires that it be governed by both positive and negative feedbacks which respond to the desired condition or target. Since we conduct our day-to-day affairs through the medium of money, that means implementing legislation that harnesses market forces. In other words the way to curb the use of energy is to tax it. But it is not quite as simple as that.

The problem with taxation of fuels is that energy has for long been so cheap. Recall the observation we made in Chapter 5 that one day's *work* effort[3] from a human being could be bought for about 5 pence. To tax fuels sufficiently to curb their use would cause dismay amongst the population and greatly distort our economies and, in the developed world, undermine our incredibly high material standard of living. What is more, most people expect this standard to keep on rising, and would vote out any government that failed to deliver. Those governments, such as the British and the French, that have raised taxes on motor fuels to the highest levels worldwide, have incurred the wrath of hauliers and farmers who have used people power to blockade ports and refineries, winning some concessions. One such blockade in the UK in September 2000 almost caused the country to run dry of fuel.

Such high taxation of transport fuels has not succeeded in stopping the growth in demand. The head of BP-Amoco in the UK stated on television that in his company's experience the demand for motor fuel was unaffected by price at the pumps. This is not surprising. Even at 85 pence per litre, one litre brings you the *work* potential of 143 human beings for one hour.[4] What a bargain!

Cheap energy has naturally encouraged the development of an energy-intensive life-style which few now want to relinquish. In these circumstances governments pin their hopes on energy conservation as a way of reducing energy use. But this has proved less successful than expected, for the plain fact is that when we get more for less, it is human nature simply to enjoy the fruits thereof by finding new ways of consuming what we save. Thus house insulation encourages whole rather than partial house central heating; hot rather than warm rooms. More efficient car engines allow us to move from small to larger or zippier cars without an economic penalty. Cut-price liquor increases consumption; witness the marketing concept known as the happy hour. Politicians may take comfort from the fact that the energy use per unit of GDP is going down, but it is a mistake to assume this is due to conservation of energy. A great deal is due to the relatively higher growth of the service sector where energy intensity is roughly half compared to manufacturing. Energy use continues to rise ineluctably.

At the same time even at the present 'cheap' price of fuel, there are many for whom it is genuinely too expensive. Most affected are those in remoter rural communities without adequate public transport. For someone on the UK minimum wage, travelling 20 miles each way to and from work in a small car absorbs 15% of his or her pre-tax income, without even taking account of the car's maintenance. The spread, too, of modern supermarket and hypermarket retailing has left the rural hinterland without its traditional local facilities or sources of income, and so people must travel simply in order to survive. Moreover most in this group have lower incomes than the urban average. Also seriously affected by the cost of fuels are pensioners, unemployed, and those on minimum wages. Energy may be cheap, and though a litre of fuel (untaxed) may generate 35 MJ for an outlay of 30pence, the modest heating of a small home in northern Europe requires about 50,000 MJ a year.[5] For those on the minimum wage that adds up to 5% of their post-tax income. For UK pensioners it is about 12%.

For people in the developing countries the problems are even greater because development implies bringing in machines to replace labour.

Whereas in most countries income tax is progressive, graded according to income, fuel prices are the same for all. Fuel poverty is an acknowledged condition. However anyone on the average European wage or above can easily afford fuels at present prices.[6] At the executive level of income the cost is a triviality. All this seems to point to the need for a gradation in fuel prices or a subsidy to the less well-off and those in remoter communities. While this need is partially recognised in government circles, it seems that its implementation faces insuperable bureaucratic obstacles. There is always the fear in the Treasury that people will find a legal way of avoiding tax. But there are better ways of achieving equity, as we shall demonstrate later in this chapter.

This is still but half the story. Europe is in competition for exports with the rest of the world. The US government barely taxes energy at all, putting their manufacturers at a distinct advantage, and this is part of the explanation why so many goods and services are cheaper in North America than in Europe.

So if energy use is to be curbed on a national basis we need a way that does not hamper competitiveness or penalise the poor.

Let's start by laying out the parameters of a desirable fuel taxation policy.

- It should reduce fossil fuel use.
- It should not disadvantage the poorer sections of the population.
- It should not disadvantage those living in remote or rural communities where public transport and service facilities are scarce.

- It should encourage the consumer to use fuel as efficiently as technically possible.
- It should leave industry with a level playing field for competition.
- It should stimulate the autonomous growth of renewable energy systems.

As taxation stands today these objectives are mutually incompatible. We present three proposals to solve that paradox: Personal Energy Rights, Unitax and Ulitax. Unitax is the most radical, and would have to be implemented on an Europe-wide basis for every country within the Union. The other two have the advantage that they could be implemented independently by any country.

Personal Energy Rights

In this approach we espouse the idea of a stakeholder economy where every citizen is endowed by government with an equal share of the national energy cake. To be useful to the individual citizen this energy right has to acquire a value and that value must be legitimately tradable. Here is how it could be done. Each year the government specifies the maximum amount of *primary* energy that will be allowed to flow into the economy. It is important to note that that limit is *primary* energy, not fuels, and does not apply to renewable energy sources. Here is how it would work:

The government's target would be dictated by many factors, but one can imagine that with the objective of meeting its obligations under the 1997 Kyoto Protocol on greenhouse gas emissions each government might specify a target that was slightly lower than the past rate of consumption. This would not be just some ministerial sound-bite. This would be for real. This target or maximum permitted consumption would be equally shared amongst the country's adult population in the form of a Personal Energy Right (PER). Thus a PER is so many GJ of energy per person per year. There is a case for a small energy share for children, perhaps graded by age.

Essential to this scheme is that the government will *not* tax energy or fuels, other than applying value-added tax where required by the rules of the European Union.

The government's target consumption will be achieved by making it a legal obligation on the part of the fuel distribution companies to acquire by purchase enough PERs from the public equal to the fuels they wish to market.

There now exists a market consisting of buyers (the energy companies) and sellers (the public) of a single unique good whose market size is constrained. PERs therefore have a monetary value set by demand, supply being finite. The government has no role to play in the resulting price of a PER. The value of these PERs will not be redeemable by exchanging energy units for goods and fuel. That would be cumbersome. Instead they will be legally tradable for money, and so will have an exchange value and thus represent a tax-free income.

Exchange facilities will naturally develop to facilitate trading in PERs. These could be banks or bureaux de change. Very likely a futures market will evolve. Given the large number of holders of PERs (for example in the UK there are 49 million adults) there are enough actors to ensure the optimum interaction between supply and demand to determine a fair price for a PER. That price will collectively depend on the degree to which the public responds to the potential for energy conservation. The government, for its part, could enter the market and buy and sell PERs to maintain a stable price, just as it does with bonds. One would expect the going rate for PERs to be widely disseminated in the media and on the internet.

What would be the effect of this arrangement on the individual citizen? In the first place the price of fuels will rise substantially. However if an individual's requirements are less than the amount of the PER, his or her fuel costs are subsidised by the value of that PER. What is lost financially by way of extra price is made up in the sale value of the PER. Suppose, for example, the price settled out at one penny per MJ (let us call it an *energy claim* of one penny per MJ), then taking the example of the UK (assuming a modest reduction in consumption compared to 2000), a PER would amount to 190,000 MJ, tradable for £1900. In other words every citizen has a tax-free income of £1900. And who pays the money? It is the fuel distribution companies who in turn recover it from the public through the price they charge for fuels.

Now 190,000 MJ represents the national average energy consumption. Those on low incomes or economically inactive will use less, and so in spite of the fact that all fuel prices will have risen by one penny per MJ they will still be better off financially.[7] Those who are active economically will be net losers, but since they have higher than average incomes, can afford it. It will be for each person to decide how or whether to economise in fuel use. In effect a consumer-driven cascade of money from the rich down to the poor has been created without any government intervention! Figure 9.1 depicts these effects as an influence diagram.

PERs offer a protection against inflation for, with a constraint on energy supply in force, any increase in money incomes will push up the market price of a PER (see again Figure 9.1) and thus its value to the low energy user.

It has been suggested that one result of the PER system would be that imports would become cheaper than home-produced goods and fuel. But there is no reason why, like value-added tax (VAT), an *energy claim* should not be rebated on exports and applied to imports. This is dealt with in greater detail in the section below entitled Unitax.

Personal Energy Rights partially meet the £77 per week citizen's income proposed by the New Economics Foundation.[8] Some advocates, such as James Robertson of that organisation,[9] propose both an energy tax and a land rent tax.

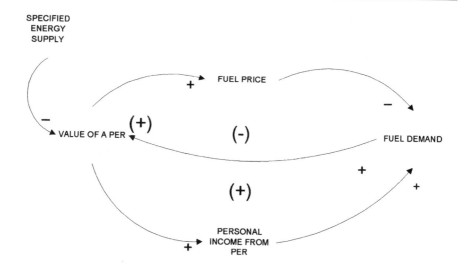

SPECIFIED
ENERGY
SUPPLY

FUEL PRICE

+

−

VALUE OF A PER   (+)   (-)   FUEL DEMAND

−

(+)

+

+

PERSONAL
INCOME FROM
PER

+

Figure 9.1: An influence diagram depicting the effect of Personal Energy Rights.

However a land tax is to all intents and purposes subsumed within an energy tax. Here's how: a parcel of land lying unused implies that no economic activity is taking place on it. Hence it will draw no energy tax. As soon as it is used, whether by a farmer to grow crops or a developer to build homes or an enterprise to build a factory, then these activities will use energy and hence pay tax.

It is important to note that only the individual citizen is furnished with an energy right. Businesses are not. It may be argued that it would be simpler to give every adult £1900 and be done with it. But this overlooks the essential aspect of feedback embodied in PERs. Whereas as individuals we may resent paying fuel tax to the government, we can hardly complain when the 'tax' is created by our own consumption and re-distributed amongst ourselves. The feedbacks that influence our personal and corporate economic decisions will change dramatically. To get the most value out of our income or sales it will now be more advantageous to choose the least energy-intensive products (see Table 9.1 below) or economise on travel and heating. The rich, being more energy-intensive, will be making a greater than usual contribution to the national exchequer. There will no longer be clever loop-holes by which they can avoid taxation.

With this system energy companies, having bought the right to distribute fuel, have a huge incentive to process primary energy into fuel at the highest possible technical efficiency. This is good from every point of view. In a competitive market it is where increased profit potential lies.

The benefits of introducing PERs

• Householders will have a huge incentive to save energy, either through the life-style they adopt or by investing in home energy conservation measures. See Table 9.1 for the energy intensity of various activities. Most fuels now being more expensive, cost-benefit analyses will favour investments in energy-saving measures that would previously have been considered uneconomic.

• The PER system encourages personal and corporate investment in renewable energy since it will not be necessary to acquire PERs in order to distribute fuels sourced from renewable energy. As the fraction of the renewable contribution to the national supply increases the value of a PER and the price of fuels will fall. Thus the government may be able to meet its international environmental obligations in a relatively painless way..

• Governments can engineer a fall in energy demand by cutting the permitted energy supply. This could help to keep down international oil prices.

• Reduced energy use will cut pollution.

Table 9.1: Energy intensity of selected products in the Netherlands in 1990, converted to GJ/£. Source: Wilting.[10]

Low-intensive

banking 2

business services 10

construction 12

beverages 17

agriculture 25

———AVERAGE———

textiles 27

paper manufacture 40

basic metals 60

basic chemicals 85

High-intensive

Mechanism

There remains the mechanism for distributing a PER to every adult citizen. This could be by smart card or a national data bank. The holder of a PER is free to choose when to sell part or all of his or her rights. In the initial year or two the government would have to intervene to maintain a relatively even price. Indeed it might be better to issue the PERs monthly, and even stagger the issue alphabetically according to surnames: A-E in the first week, F-M in the second and so on. As the civil servants are wont to say, the devil is in the detail, but in a cyber-proficient economy it should not be too difficult to iron out the problems. Finally, instead of allocating to all adults, the rights might be restricted to those who are on the electoral roll. This would encourage people who have evaded their responsibilities, to rejoin society.

Unitax

Unified indirect taxation – or *unitax* for short – was put forward some twenty years ago. It is the brainchild of a manufacturer and businessman, that is to say someone who understands at first hand not only the preoccupations of the employee, but the roles, trials and tribulations of being an employer, a producer and an exporter. His name is Farel Bradbury. Support for unitax has blossomed over the years. There is now a Unitax Association whose chairman is Lord Duncan McNair.

Bradbury, a man given to puns, called his first publication on unitax the *Joules of Wealth*.[11] In 1990 a group of unitax enthusiasts chose to fight a UK parliamentary by-election in Monmouth as a way of spreading the word. On the election literature voters were offered a plastic teaspoon with the following verse:

The economic spoon
My story spans a million years
extended birth,
ephemeral life,
You tore a hundred thousand Joules
from mother earth
to stir your tea,
and tomorrow, when I'm done, you see
this value gone forever from your planetary account.
But, before I go, I render Nature's bill –
you owe this to your environment and will pay
eventually

FB 1981

The Labour candidate won.

In a unitaxed economy, once fully implemented, all labour taxes would be replaced by a tax on all *primary* energy entering the economy. The impact of such a radical change in taxation is not as drastic as might at first sight appear. Primary energy, you will recall, is raw, unrefined stuff that needs treatment to be turned into marketable fuels and feedstock for petrochemicals. The proposed tax is a caloric tax on its energy content;[12] so much per Joule,[13] and identical for all primary fuels: coal, oil, gas nuclear heat, but not electricity as it is not a primary fuel. Thereafter the price of energy filters down through the economy affecting the price of any activity or production that uses primary energy (which includes electricity). There is no need for any further government interference. Just as monetary value is added through human skill as materials and services progress through the economy, so also is energy embodied during the processes of transforming raw materials into finished products. This applies equally to manufactured goods and services, from making households goods to delivering a pizza to your door. Under the existing system of labour taxation the more labour involved (since labour is taxed) the more the goods cost. Under unitax there is no tax on labour.

As we shall see, to replace all taxes on labour with a tax on primary energy would make primary energy very expensive by current standards, but still cheap in terms of what it can do for you. An obvious objection, so often raised, is that unitax would make exports uncompetitive. But there is no reason why, as Bradbury proposes, this tax should not be rebated at the frontier just as value-added tax is rebated today, and imposed on imports. We shall expand on this later.

Unitax would be phased in gradually, initially replacing income tax. Eventually there would be no more income tax, no more value-added tax or sales tax, no more corporation tax, no more social security levies for either employees or employers. It would be a different world, economically and environmentally.

Is this not a new Utopia for employers? Just imagine the attraction of running an enterprise in an economy where there were no tax inspectors, no taxes to pay, no complex accounting associated with employing people. The attractions of relocating to low-wage economies would pale before such blandishments.

Of course alarm bells will already be ringing in readers' heads. What would a high price of energy do to people's living standards and life-styles? Well, it would certainly alter the way they spend their incomes. But as we shall show it would not impoverish anyone.

An example of unitax at work

Let's try out unitax on a particular economy, the United Kingdom in 1999, the latest year for which there are reliable statistics. Largely through taxes on labour the UK government raised £288 billion:[14] £92 billion from income tax, £32 billion from companies (corporation tax), £54 billion from social security contributions (employers, employees and self-employed), and £62 billion from VAT. We shall not include the £48 billion from various levies such as duty on hydrocarbons which are not labour taxes. The country consumed 260 million tonnes of oil-equivalent primary energy[15] (10,900 million GJ). There were also some supplies from renewable sources such as wind, biomass and hydro-electricity. They are not included, but are very small. The official statistics do not fully take account of the energy embodied in imports, and they ignore the solar energy flows captured by agriculture and forestry. We can however say, within about 5% accuracy, that the national primary energy consumption was 10,900 million GJ; that is about four tonnes of oil equivalent per person or a volume of oil equal to that of a typical bottle bank (for discarded bottles), though only enough to fly a jumbo jet 180 kilometres.

The unitax rate on primary energy would be set by the government. In 1999, to yield the required revenue of £288 billion would have required a taxation rate on primary energy entering the economy of £26 per GJ (2.6 pence per MJ). – £288 billion divided by 10,900 billion GJ. This is £1086 per tonne of oil equivalent. Whew! Currently oil sells on the international (untaxed) market at just over $30 per barrel or $220 (£150) per tonne.[16] Can any economy sustain such a price shock?

Not suddenly. And, of course, the tax has to be fiscally neutral. It would not be like the price hike engineered by the OPEC cartel twenty-five years ago which shook the world to its roots. Once implemented in full the average UK adult citizen (at 1999 levels of income) would be in possession of £4900 more spending power, while the cost of the energy implicit in the average life-style would have risen from £1600 to £5700, or £4100 more. Thus the average taxpayer is no worse off; even a little better.

Phasing in unitax

As we have said, unitax would be phased in gradually. Table 9.2 shows the unitax rate resulting from the removal of any one of the four current national labour taxes. To give a benchmark, the likely effect on the price of electricity is listed in the right-hand column. In noting the electricity figure remember that electricity is generated by using some form of primary energy, which will carry a primary unitax.

A problem often raised by objectors is that since unitax would encourage better use of energy, fuel consumption would fall and therefore government revenue. The tax is said to erode its own base. This is true. Eventually, however, the rate will stabilise as the positive and negative feedbacks balance each other out.

The many effects of unitax

In addition to the benefits listed earlier for personal energy rights there are other effects to be expected from the implementation of unitax.

Table 9.2: The effect of replacing 'labour' taxes with unitax. Figures are for the United Kingdom in 1999 expressed in 1999 pounds and GJ of energy.

'Labour' tax to be replaced	1999 Tax raised billion £	Unitax rate resulting, pence/MJ	Effect on electricity price, status quo = 1, assuming no improvement in efficiency of generation
value-added tax (VAT) only	62	0.57	1.8
income tax only	92	0.84	2.05
corporation tax only	32	0.29	1.4
social security contributions only	54	0.49	1.75
income tax + VAT + social security contributions	208	1.9	3.3

• Incomes are (eventually) tax-free, which increases freedom of choice to the consumer.

• The tax on motor fuels barely rises. It is already (in the year 2001) 1.7 pence per MJ in countries such as the UK and France.

• Since renewable energy systems are not subject to unitax, householders have enormous incentives to build solar energy capture devices into their houses or on their land. This is good both for the economic welfare of the individual and for the long-term durability of the national economy.

• House-building costs can be expected to fall, since the energy intensity of construction is about 50% of the average of the economy as a whole (Table 9.1), and labour, the most expensive item in building, is now tax-free.

• As unitax is rebated at the frontier, exporters will find, if they do their sums, that it makes them more, not less, internationally competitive.

• There is a level playing field because imports are taxed on their embodied energy content. This is a much simpler procedure than generally appreciated, as those familiar with the techniques of energy analysis will know. The complexity of the present tariff system requires a 1400 page guide in the case of the UK.

• As unitax is a caloric tax, it bears equally on all types of primary energy.

• Electricity, being a secondary fuel, is taxed through the primary energy source used for its generation. Even the most modest technical advance in energy efficiency would have a significant effect on the price. A mere 2% would reduce it by a penny a unit. The best technologies today can generate electricity at 47%

thermal efficiency, which would take 5 pence a unit off the price.

• Unitax encourages the recycling of depleted uranium in reactors, and so ultimately reduces the amount of radioactive waste. The position of nuclear energy here as a means of generating electricity is interesting. What tax exactly does one put upon uranium? Logic would demand that it be on the potential fissile energy that could be liberated were all the fissile fuel to be used.

• Unitax is the same for all. This may seem regressive. However it draws more tax from those whose life-styles are energy intensive, and who travel more. That symbol of affluence, the all-terrain four wheel drive vehicle so much in evidence in the city of London, will contribute particularly generously.

• Unlike the situation with 'labour' taxes, no amount of creative accounting can help to avoid tax, though no doubt some clever minds will devote their energies to just such an objective. Much good may it do them.

• Since the tax is unevadable, it nets the criminal classes, the black economy, the money-fixers and the drug barons, not to mention the tourists visiting the country.

• With less bureaucracy associated with employment, labour will be hired more readily. At the same time some labour may become cheaper since take-home pay will be greater.

• Profits of enterprises can now be increased by intelligent conservation of energy rather than by down-sizing the labour force.

• Unitax provides a government with a sensitive lever on economic management. The unitax rate can be changed instantly, with immediate effect throughout the economy.

• Because unitax is levied on primary energy, and since this enters the economy at relatively few points, monitoring the tax will require a corps of not more than a few hundred inspectors. Compare this to the 120,000 people in the UK currently engaged in monitoring 'labour' taxation whose wages absorb 4.5% of the total revenue – some £9 billion in 1997. And then there is the saving of not having to engage tax accountants.

• Labour-intensive products like organic vegetables are relatively cheaper.

Has unitax struck a chord?

Unitax has attracted interest and support at many international conferences. Curiously, given the inherent advantage to export prices, exporters have not yet grasped its potential. Of course, there is always opposition to any rise in energy prices, which if nothing else demonstrates the importance of energy. UK government ministers, even when they have publicly invited suggestions from the public, have not shown any curiosity to know more. Of course, all suggestions go straight to the Treasury, where their fate is pre-ordained by a team of people who can only think in financial terms. The same may be said for the European Commission. Lateral thinking on sustainability is slow to take root.

One must always bear in mind that whatever the taxation system in place, all costs finally fall upon the citizen in his or her role as consumer and taxpayer. This is where the impact should be considered. Initial public reaction is bound to be hostile, for that most immediate of impacts, the price of home heating, would rise. Yet if unitax were phased in gradually, say with income tax removed first, and with proper provision for the less well-off and remote communities, the public would scarcely notice any change in prices. It has to be marketed as part of a Europe-wide plan to create a durable economy.

So what would the effect be on the average family? Taking UK data for 1997, the average spent on home heating, lighting and cooking was £8.70 a week for the poorest decal (tenth) of home incomes. Here the average occupancy is 1.3 persons per home; that is, £6.70 per person per week. Households in the richest decal spend £18 per week, but there the average occupancy rate is 3.1 persons per home, so that the per capita cost is £5.80. To put these sums in perspective, the average spent on cars per family was £46 per week! The average household expenditure on home energy was £12.50 per week. Under full unitax (appropriate to 1997), gas would become six times more expensive, fuel oils a little less. Electricity prices could be three times as much. But however bad it looks at first sight, the *net* impact is zero provided the consumer responds intelligently to the new feedbacks. For an average family heating costs would rise to £32 per week (annualised) and £14 for electricity – an increase of £34. This is the same as the current average income tax, social security payments and VAT, which now no longer have to be paid.

Though under unitax transport fuels will be expensive, the difference will hardly be noticed as they are already highly taxed. However those who currently enjoy tax-free transport fuels, such as farmers and fishermen, will now find good reason to think about what machinery they use or how far afield it is worth sailing[17]. This will not put them at an economic disadvantage, for if their output costs are higher as a result they will be passed on to the consumer. At the same time competing imported agricultural products will bear a tax based on their embodied energy. This situation may be expected to offer some advantage to the beleaguered, less favourable farming areas. One spin-off is that fishing boats from ports distant from the fishing grounds would not find the journey economically worthwhile, thus relieving pressure on fish stocks.

Providing for those on low incomes

When faced with the unitax proposal politicians naturally point to its unfavourable impact on those with low incomes. As with any taxation system such people need help. It cannot be beyond our wit to sort out this problem. A suggestion from one quarter is a citizen's basic wage for all,[18] an end that can also be achieved with the concept of Personal Energy Rights already presented. Yet another way is to rebate the tax on electricity on the first so many units consumed per household. This would be simple to administer. For example, if the first 2000 kWh/y per household were rebated that would be equal to a subsidy of £300 a year.

There are several reasons for choosing electricity:

• There are many diverse sources of fuels. A rebate on all of them would be a bureaucratic maze. Hence the range of fuel on which the rebate is made available must be limited.

• Everyone has to use electricity, whereas there is ample room for substitution in respect of other fuels.

• A household's electricity is billed by one supplier, so that providing a rebate on the first 2000 kWh per year is a trivial billing procedure.

• The poorer sections of the population tend to use electricity for heating as domestic appliances are cheap to buy and install (though expensive to use). Hence they above all others should enjoy the reduced tax on the threshold consumption.

The other issue is that with rural and island communities already facing unreasonably high transport costs any additional tax is unacceptable. There is no reason however why a subsidy on transport fuels should not be legislated, say, one that is inversely proportional to the population density.

Fuel-based local unitax – Ulitax

To the four forms of taxation listed in Table 9.2 should be added yet another: the tax levied by local administrations for the provision of services like water, sewage, lighting, social services, education and so on. Revenue is usually raised through some form of property tax, a procedure that is full of anomalies. Could energy taxation at the local level offer a fairer and more effective method? Let's look at this possibility. It has come to be called *Ulitax*. This idea won one of the authors and Farel Bradbury, the inspiration behind ulitax, the first prize in 1990 for the best social invention of the year, offered by Anita Roddick of Body Shop and the Institute for Social Inventions.

Here each local authority raises its revenue from a caloric[19] tax on *fuels* (not primary energy as with unitax) sold within its jurisdiction. The mechanism for this already exists, since all businesses have to collect and remit VAT or (in the USA) sales taxes. Ulitax provides the same valuable feedbacks as unitax, but at the local level. The effect, as we shall see, is to shift much of the tax burden from households, industry and commerce onto private transport. Like unitax, ulitax is unavoidable and provides a simple, low-cost way of raising revenue. Electricity would be taxed on its heat equivalent which is 3.6 MJ per unit (= 1 kWh).

Table 9.3 gives some idea of how ulitax might impact upon five very different cities in different parts of the world.

Table 9.3: The Ulitax required to replace conventional taxes in several cities.

city	estimated average energy use, GJ/capita	cost of local government US$/capita	Ulitax – local currency/MJ	additional cost of motor fuel UK pence /litre	additional cost of electricity UK pence /kWh
Vienna	102	5605	ATS 0.7	109	10.0
Hong Kong	116	5087	HK$ 0.3	95	9.7
Moscow	185	388	$0.00186*	1	1
Pune	9.4	37	INR 0.12	1	0.64
Winnipeg	240	1460	0.009 CAN $	7	1.5
Edinburgh	180	1882	£ 0.015	50	5
* rouble exchange rates change rapidly					

Who gains and who loses from this form of taxation? Table 9.3 alone cannot answer this question. One needs more detailed information on cities than is generally available. However there are to hand data for two UK cities; Edinburgh and Newcastle (Table 9.4). It shows that business and commerce gain a little, while households gain enormously. Transport fuel costs rise substantially. This is entirely consistent with a strategy to cut fossil fuel use and to discourage car commuting.

Thus in Edinburgh an oil-based fuel like petrol would cost an additional 9 pence a litre, while in Newcastle it would have added 6.5 pence. Electricity would cost an additional 2.9 pence per unit in Edinburgh, but only 2 pence more in Newcastle. Even so, Edinburgh's householders would be £47 million better off, and Newcastle's £17.1 million. The losers are the private car drivers, who would pay £52 million more a year for their pleasures in Edinburgh. The figure for Newcastle cannot be calculated from the available data.

Table 9.4: Who gains, who loses? The effect of a caloric fuel tax in Edinburgh and Newcastle in the year 1990 to replace property taxes. Source; Resource Use Institute, 1991.

In 1990 Newcastle would have required a caloric fuel tax of 0.545 pence per MJ

	fuel use: million MJ	caloric tax million £	local taxation in 1990	change, million £
Commerce & industry				
for heating, lighting etc.	9125	49.7	60	-10.3
Transport	5137	28.0	nil	+28.0
Domestic housing	7873	42.9	60	-17.1
All activities	**22099**	**120.6**	**120.6**	**no change**

In 1990 Edinburgh would have required a caloric fuel tax of 0.793 pence per MJ*

	fuel use: million MJ	caloric tax, million £	local taxation in 1990	change, million £
Business & commerce:				
light goods vehicles	790	6.0	nil	+ 6.0
heavy goods vehicles	2520	19.2	nil	+ 19.2
railways	480	3.7	nil	+ 3.7
premises: heat & light	- - -	- - -	197.7	– 197.7
operational fuel	21500	163.8	nil	+ 163.8
Private: dwellings	13900	105.9	153.1	– 47.2
motoring	6800	52.0	nil	+ 52.0
All activities	**46000**	**350.8**	**350.8**	**no change**

* In this table existing excise taxes on fuels and vehicles are assumed still to be in place, but this need not be so.

No tax would be levied on privately collected fuels, like scavenged wood or domestic solar collectors. Ulitax is likely to induce an accelerated investment in solar capture systems by home owners, which is sound economics for the country as a whole.

Local authority costs can be expected to fall, as there is no need for property assessors or mailing annual property rates bills.

Those on low incomes could be helped by having a threshold electricity consumption, below which no tax was levied, just as was suggested for unitax. For example this would be worth £55 a year per household in Edinburgh, £19 in Newcastle. The local government would have the power to alter the threshold, and in this way could compete with neighbouring local governments to render its tax competitive.

The effect of a threshold of 2000 kWh/y in Edinburgh would have been (in 1990) to raise the caloric tax on the remainder of the fuel use by 4.8%.

Differences between neighbouring local authorities

What happens if one local government area has a lower caloric ulitax than a neighbouring one? Will not motorists cross the 'border' to buy cheaper fuel? Suppose the caloric tax in the next region were 10% lower, then its petrol would be 3.1 pence a litre cheaper. According to the Automobile Association, the real cost of driving a car is at least 15 pence a kilometre so that to fill a tank of 45 litres, the maximum diversion that would be economical is 12-14 kilometres, *there and back*. Cigarettes are cheaper in New Jersey than New York, but the bridges over the Hudson are not clogged with smokers seeking cheap fags.

Conclusion

The three energy taxation systems put forward are all administratively feasible and fiscally neutral. They operate within the dicta of the free market. They introduce powerful feedbacks that would push the economy (and the consumer) in the direction of creating a durable economy and environment. None is perfect, just as no taxation system is perfect.

It is going to require tremendous political will on the part of government to make a change. One can imagine the entrenched opposition from tax accountants and inspectors, who would largely become redundant, or from long-distance car commuters whose costs would rise. Trucking companies have little to fear. But the important point is that the people as a whole would not suffer and the economy and environment would benefit. Who knows, durability might become a reality.

But there is a sad postscript to all this. When any of these ideas are floated amongst the body public, they draw shock and horror. Yet the very same people, both citizens and politicians, will agree that energy use has to be reduced. When one challenges them to come up with their proposal, they have none, bar the old remedy of energy efficiency. In spite of the evidence of the rebound effect, they still cling on to this hope. Yet the facts are that energy use is ineluctably rising. Those countries that have managed slight reductions in carbon dioxide output (mostly in Europe) have done so by switching the generation of electricity from coal to natural gas. That can only take us so far. It is not a permanent solution. Feedback and economic instruments are the key, and energy taxation in place of labour taxation is surely worth a serious examination.

Notes

1   In order to consider like with like, one has to take into account those provisions that in some countries are provided by the state through taxes which in other countries are provided at a fee by private enterprise. Health insurance is a prime example. In computing tax rates the authors have calculated the total outlay by an individual to gain all the usual services from the state, such as health services, education, roads etc.

2   *Energy analysis in technology assessment*, M. Slesser, 1974, Technology Assessment, 2, No. 3 pp 201-208.

3   Just to remind the reader that *work* and heat are different.

4   In round figures, 35 MJ is the amount of heat that would generate 10 kWh of electricity, that is 10,000 watts for one hour. As pointed out in Chapter 5, an average fit adult can generate about 70 w atts of work. 10,000 divided by 70 is 143.

5   This is the price paid by households. Fishermen buying in large quantities pay as little as 20 pence a litre.

6   'Present prices' are when these words were written, July 2001. Two years earlier crude oil was selling at a third of this price, the lowest ever in real terms. In the authors view the July 2001 price is likely to be maintained for many years, though with some fluctuation, and then will rise further.

7   Motor fuels, on the other hand, would be cheaper. At one penny per MJ, petrol in the UK which as at November 2000 costs 85 pence, would drop to 65 pence.

8   See the CD-Rom published by the New Economics Foundation issued in February, 2000: www.neweconomics.org.

9   *Benefits & Taxes: A Radical Strategy,* J. Robertson, 1994, New Economics Foundation, London.

10   *An energy perspective on economic activities*, H. Wilting, 1996, doctorate thesis, Institute for Environment and Energy, University of Groningen, The Netherlands.

11   *The Delight of Resource Economic,*1986 and *The Joules of Wealth*, 1988, F. Bradbury, Hydatum Publishers, 70 Silverdale Rd, Tunbridge Wells, Kent.

12   Caloric means based on the heat potential of the fuel. 'Energy content' is a very loose phrase, justly to be criticised by those who work with energy. What is meant is the potential heat that can be released by the energy source. The amount that can be turned into *work* depends on   the technology and the skill of the user.

13   A Joule is a unit of energy – refer to Glossary.

14   Table 1.7.5, *UK National Accounts*, 1998. H.M. Stationery Office.

15   One tonne of oil is assumed in UK government statistics to have a heat potential of 41.87 GJ. In reality it varies from crude to crude. In this book a tonne oil equivalent is taken as 41.8 GJ.

16   What will be the future price of oil? The financial community tends to think it will fall, the technological community that it will rise. The authors believe it will oscillate, but rise in the long haul.

17   Nowadays with the ever smaller potential yield due to over-fishing even a small prawn fisher will use 500 litres of fuel a day.

18   A very strong case has been made in a discussion paper of the New Economics Foundation (1994) by the former civil servant James Robertson: *Benefits and Taxes; a radical strategy.'*

19   Caloric means based on the heat potential of the fuel. Since fuels are often used wastefully such a tax would encourage more considered use, and encourage energy conservation practices.

10

Investing for the future

Ah, love! Could thou and I with Fate conspire
to grasp this sorry scheme of things entire,
Would not we shatter it to bits – and then
remould it nearer to the Heart's desire?
FROM THE RUBAIYAT OF OMAR KHAYYAM

What is your desire for the future? It is too easy to say a world without strife, without hunger, one of justice and equality. This we can all agree to. Whether such a world can be built to order is another question. The point to be made here is that no matter what sort of world we aspire to, whatever wonderful inventions lie in store, we cannot escape the physical limitations imposed by nature. The one constraint that neither vision nor hope can get around are the laws of thermodynamics which dictate how much energy it takes to do something, make something or get somewhere. This was touched upon in Chapter 5.

This constraint rarely surfaces when futurists offer us their visions. So many of them implicitly assume that the economy will grow and grow. Of course there will be remarkable developments in technology of all sorts, but it is all too easy to ignore the energy implications. While it is perfectly true that it takes very, very little energy to operate computers and telecommunications,[1] the whole purpose behind knowledge-based communication is to manage the human input to production and distribution more effectively. However, if anything, cyberspace has increased the use of energy by generating additional activity.

This chapter explores how we may get around the coming energy and environment limitations, for it is within those parameters that the future will be moulded.

We cannot use economic models for this purpose, because economics has no paradigm for energy, that is to say it has no way of forecasting energy prices. The conventional way out of this bind is to generate scenarios of the future; the sort that say 'what if...?', as in 'what if the economic growth rate were 3% over the next two years?' or 'assuming that energy prices rise 2% per year, what would be the outcome?' An economic model is then pressed into service and fed these assumptions. This will spell out the consequences, but they will have little meaning as no one can know if the assumptions are justified. Anyway they are unable to look far enough ahead to spot up-coming problems. And if no impending energy constraints have been factored in then the forecast will be misleading even if the other assumptions turn out to be correct.

Scenario building has quite a fan club. It certainly allows the mind enormous freedom. In a mid-1990s publication by the European Commission twelve economists were invited to visualise a range of possible futures. In one scenario they imagined supersonic solar-powered jets providing weekend breaks in Rio de Janeiro for bored Europeans. Whether the idea appeals or not, even a superficial examination of the underlying physics demonstrates its impossibility. The trouble with using money as a basis for looking into the future is that a policy which on paper appears economically feasible may be physically impossible.

This being so, why not take our earlier suggestion of determining the physical outcome of proposed scenarios to see whether they are practicable in the first place? Natural capital accounting models[2] offer a way of doing this. For those who wish to plunge deeper into this methodology, Appendix 3 gives a description.

Here the visionary explores his or her ideas to see what effect they will have on the overall growth of the economy and the pressure on the envionment. Ideas have to be expressed as policies. These may be social, technological or environmental, possibly derived from prior economic studies or simply from brain-storming.

The model is then run forward into the future and spells out the consequences in physical, not monetary terms. This is physical rather than monetary econometrics, what is called Physical Econometric Dynamic Assessment (PEDA).

It should be remembered that many actions are physically possible on a limited basis only. For example, though we have the technology, energy and capital to set up a space station on Mars, a back-of-the-envelope calculation is enough to show that we cannot emigrate there in large numbers. The physical requirements are too great. People who plan satellite launches work out the physical requirements first, and then the economic consequences. If the economic consequences are unacceptable, then it's back to the drawing board. This approach restores to economics its appropriate role.

Let's take an issue that engages many minds. Can nuclear energy production of electricity with its inherent dangers be abandoned? Germany, Sweden and Austria have voted to do so. Natural capital accounting might be used to explore two obvious options: cutting out nuclear electricity and making do with less electricity, or replacing nuclear with alternative means of generation. If the latter, then the technologies have to be specified.[3] They could, for example, be based on coal, natural gas or wind turbines. Whatever the choice their use implies prior investment, that is to say HMC (human-made capital expressed in physical terms). The model takes account of the HMC diverted to these purposes, and spells out the effect on economic growth sector by sector. It further spells out the reduced flow of radioactive wastes, the increased carbon dioxide output, and so forth.

More often than not the outcome is not what you might expect. In the case of building renewable energy systems, to take one example, the very large consequent diversion of HMC has the effect of cutting back on material welfare. Again, those who though wishing to abandon nuclear energy want to maintain existing material standards of living, often pin their arguments on the potential benefits of the more efficient use of energy. However raising the efficiency of energy use requires prior investment, that is diversion of HMC to an extent that may also slow down growth in unexpected sectors. There are never any free lunches.

A typical natural capital accounting model will have as many as 2000 equations, and generate almost as many output data.[4] The user has to select those which inform best. It is sometimes found that a particular set of policies results first in growth, then a peaking followed by decline. Whether this, or any other outcome, is judged good or bad is for the user to decide and if bad, the user must then use the output of the model to visualise an alternative policy. Models of this type are a kind of litmus test to check the physical practicality of money-based models and armchair visions. They impose no ideas of their own. To give some insight into how they can be used, here are three logical targets for the EU that were examined as part of a policy study for a sustainable Europe commissioned by the European Commission.[5] Since this particular model treats the EU as if it were one single national economy, it effectively assumes a free internal market.

The targets were:
• Achieving an acceptable level of unemployment.
• Meeting the original 1997 Kyoto international protocol commitments on carbon dioxide emissions.
• Increasing the EU's self-sufficiency in energy supply.

Attaining any one of these targets calls for appropriate policies and their implementation. The reader might care to jot down on a piece of paper those that she or he considers might achieve each of these desired objectives. According to conventional thinking they might be as follows:
• Reducing unemployment: artificial stimulation of the economy by borrowing externally.

• Reducing carbon dioxide emissions: massive investment in energy conservation.

• Increasing self-sufficiency in energy: major investment in renewable energy systems for electricity generation.

These three targets using the above policies were duly explored using the model to discover the outcomes. One finds that all sorts of other developments in the economy emerge that are unexpected, often unwanted. Rather than burden the reader with a torrent of results making it almost impossible to distinguish the wheat from the chaff, the success of each of these policy studies will be judged by comparing them with a benchmark study called business-as-usual (BAU). Here it is assumed that all current policies and trends in the EU continue unchanged to 2015. Of course, such an unchanging evolution of the economy will certainly *not* come to pass. As events unfold, new initiatives, new technologies and new options will be grasped. However it is useful to be informed of what might have happened if nothing was changed. In this way, too, one can judge whether the policy under test is useful or not, and whether it goes all or part of the way to achieving the desired target. At the very least politicians can take time by the fore-lock and obviate some of the pitfalls lying ahead!

Table 10.1 summarises in terms of a few key criteria the BAU outcome for the EU's current fifteen countries (EU-15) to the year 2015 compared to 1999. In assessing it the reader should bear in mind that an omnibus model of this sort spells out the climate rather than the weather. It is not concerned with the small detail. Do not expect precise forecasts.

Table 10.1: A business-as-usual profile for the 15 countries of the EU

• Economic growth is about 2% annually.
• Manufacturing output is up 50%.
• The material standard of living is up 20%.
• Primary energy demand is up 50%.
• Carbon dioxide output is up 45%.
• Self-sufficiency in energy falls to 25%.
• Unemployment is very high, maybe even 30%

And so to looking at the policies aimed at achieving the three targets listed above.

A policy of solving unemployment by expanding the economy

Here we adopt Keynesian policies and borrow to make the economy expand faster. So far as unemployment goes, it works. Table 10.2 depicts the picture by 2015:

Table 10.2: Target of low unemployment.
- Growth rate: 40% higher than BAU.
- Manufacturing output: 90% greater than BAU.
- Material standard of living: 70% higher than BAU.
- Primary energy demand: 45% higher than BAU.
- Carbon dioxide output: 60% higher than BAU.
- Unemployment falls to 4%.

However the cost of all this is a huge rise in EU-15 external debt, exceeding the proportion of GDP laid down in the EU's Maastrict Treaty conditions for membership of the European Monetary Union.

Thus the employment objective is met, but at the expense of reduced environmental and physical sustainability. The conclusion is that non-indigenous growth is not a sustainable path, nor the right way to reduce unemployment.

A policy of cutting down carbon dioxide emissions

In this example we seek to achieve reduced carbon dioxide emissions by massive investment in energy efficiency measures. Table 10.3 depicts the outcome by 2015.

Table 10.3: Target of carbon dioxide emissions.
- Growth rate: much the same as BAU.
- Manufacturing output: about the same as BAU.
- Material standard of living: 15% less than BAU, i.e. practically no rise at all from the year 2000.
- Primary energy demand: 30% lower than BAU.
- Carbon dioxide: meets the Kyoto commitment.
- Unemployment: much the same as BAU – unacceptably high.

This strategy shows a huge improvement in output per unit energy use and a significant reduction in carbon dioxide, meeting EU commitments. However it does nothing for the curse of unemployment and the material standard of living falls.

If the perceptive reader recalls the remarks made in Chapter 7 about the rebound effect she or he may wonder at this result. What happens is that in a natural capital accounting ECCO model there is a positive feedback from material standard of living to the demand for energy by the population at large. Thus these studies automatically take account of the rebound effect.

A policy of achieving physical sustainability

In the two tests described so far EU-15 self-sufficiency in energy still declines as time passes, even with a major effort towards conservation. Could a fast-track investment programme in renewable energies improve matters? Here we assume a deliberate government-led programme of investment in renewable energy systems: a mix of wind turbine and photo-voltaic. We assume that the resulting growth in renewables will be accompanied by a learning curve halving the capital cost (HMC) per unit power by 2015. Note that such a policy would never be adopted using only economic judgements. It would be considered wildly uneconomic, at least in the early stages. Table 10.4 depicts the outcome by 2015:

Table 10.4: Fast-track investment in renewable energy systems.
- Growth rate: 45% less than BAU.
- Manufacturing output: 25% more than for the year 2000, but 11% less than BAU.
- Material standard of living: 24 % less than BAU.
- Primary energy: demand 20% less than BAU.
- Self-sufficiency in energy: better than BAU with 33% of electricity from renewable sources.
- Unemployment: even higher than BAU.

Though self-sufficiency in energy is improved, the other outcomes make this an unattractive policy. The reduced output and increased unemployment are directly due to the massive diversion of capital to investment in renewables which, because of their low load factor (see again Chapter 6), require about three times as much investment per unit output as conventional or nuclear energy sources.

What is clear from these trials is that though it is possible to solve one problem, all three cannot simultaneously be solved by the policies chosen and implemented. This alone is a useful and important insight, and provokes one to search for and explore through the model a different set of policies.

A combined evolutionary policy

Having learnt from the three policy studies, the authors used their judgement to propose a combined but less ambitious set of policies, to be introduced between 2000 and 2015. This we call an evolutionary policy.

- Introduction of combined heat and power, whereby waste heat from power stations is used as space heating in domestic and commercial buildings – 60% penetration by 2015.
- Energy conservation:
  a) autonomous (i.e. more careful use of energy) improvement of 5% by 2015.

b) investment to yield a 75% reduction in energy use per unit output.

- Measures to slow down the rate of technical change in the market services sector to half the 1997 rate of penetration, while freezing it in the non-market sector.

- Investment in renewable energy systems at such a rate as to create 10,000 jobs a year in their manufacture by 2010, increasing to 15,000 a year by 2015. The outcome by 2015 is shown in Table 10.5.

Table 10.5: A combined evolutionary policy.

- Growth rate: 17% higher than BAU.
- Manufacturing output: 48% higher than BAU.
- Material standard of living: 5% greater than BAU.
- Primary energy demand: 65% less than BAU.
- Self-sufficiency in energy: 40% (i.e. 50% better than BAU).
- Carbon dioxide output: 30% less than BAU.
- Unemployment: 5% (much better than BAU).

While the outcome is encouraging and offers a significant shift towards durability in the full sense of the word, many options remain to be explored which might produce a more satisfactory outcome.

The result of this evolutionary scenario leads one to conclude that a fully durable Europe is not beyond our grasp. However it would be to put one's head in the sand to imagine it can happen without curtailing the material standard of living in the interim. It is also hard to see how such an evolution of the EU could occur solely under market forces. Almost certainly some of the EU's holy policy cows will need modification, in particular its energy policy.

Some of the results of the above studies will puzzle readers. Why, for instance, does growth falter in certain cases? The reason is that massive investment in renewable energy systems or in energy conservation diverts HMC from economic expansion, thus diminishing the surplus for expansion. According to one's position on the political spectrum from Green to Red to Blue this may be interpreted as good, indifferent or bad. What is quite clear is that the status quo is not an option if environmental objectives and improved energy self-sufficiency are sought. It is the old story. Economic growth can solve many problems, but creates others. Durable development is the trade-off between the two. No easy solutions present themselves.[6] To attain any real progress towards durability will be a very difficult task politically with a public conditioned to believe it can be materially better off year after year.

The reader may well enquire whether the above results from the SUE natural capital accounting model are reliable. Should not the results be compared with a conventional econometric model? Only very recently have such models been made that can be run two decades into the future. Such a model is the Panta Rhei econometric input-output model created at Osnabruck University for the German economy.[7] The same integrated strategy was tested on both SUE and Panta Rhei. The results are not strictly comparable as one is a model of Germany and the other of the EU-15 average. Table 10.6 compares the two, which are seen to offer very similar predictions, especially if one recognises that such models can only spell out the broad picture, not the detail.

Table 10.6: Comparison between SUE ECCO model and Panta Rhei econometric model of an integrated scenario of several policies aimed at increasing durability by 2020.

Indicator	SUE	Econometric
GDP	+45%	+33%
material inputs	-27%	-28%
CO_2 emissions	-15%	-14%
standard of living	better	better
disposable income	less	more
unemployment rate	3% in 2020	3.3% in 2020

The wider world

The EU is one of the richest parts of the world. How fare the developing or less industrialised countries? That depends to a very considerable degree on their rate of population growth. A study using a natural capital accounting world model examined the prospects.[8] The nation states were placed in two baskets: one representing industrialised and developed nations, the other developing countries. For this second group the business-as-usual prospects were not greatly encouraging. Though standards of living rose, they remained well below that of the richer, developed world. Little convergence was observable. The two factors that had greatest impact in holding back their advancement were population increase and debt servicing. Happily birth rates are falling in the less developed countries, and latest reports from the UN state that average family size has fallen from six a few years ago to under three. China, one of the world's fastest growing and largest economies, still has a policy of encouraging one child per family.

So how do we prepare for the time when the oil runs out?

Those who espouse renewable energy, whether as an alternative to nuclear energy, to reduce greenhouse gas emissions or to provide a substitute for when the oil runs out, recognise that society should be putting something aside for that rainy day, much as we forgo income to provide us with pensions. Paul Ekins, for example, an English physicist turned economist and member of the New Economics Foundation, has argued that we should be saving (in the monetary sense) a proportion of the wealth gained from oil and gas extraction to build up a fund that can be tapped to construct renewable energy systems when oil and gas become scarce.

While the principle behind this proposition is admirable, it does not go far enough. Here's the flaw. Supposing a government agreed to such an proposition, what would happen to the money put aside? Since money cannot be stored, these funds would have to be invested in some way. If invested in the national economy, they would be locked away in manufacturing plants, leisure centres, airlines and so forth. If credited to the government they would probably be used to reduce the national debt or reduce taxes. Meanwhile the economy proceeds at its merry pace, with more and more fossil-fired electricity generators and oil refineries being built to satisfy demand. When eventually it appears urgent to build renewable energy systems to fill the looming gap in fossil supplies, who will want to buy the equity in those failing investments?

More significantly, when this situation does finally arise, energy will be getting more expensive, and so the cost of building the renewable systems will be that much more because the price of energy has a direct one-to-one effect on manufacturing costs.[9] Ekins' proposal has to be re-interpreted in physical terms. It requires that from this moment forth there be a deliberate building up of renewable energy systems on a significant scale. This is where we should be investing some of our wealth.

So is there time to build a renewable energy-based economy before the oil runs out? This is a question easily answered using a natural capital accounting model. The answer varies from economy to economy. For a densely populated country like England opposed to the expansion of nuclear energy it is 'no' unless there is a complete turnabout in society's approach to the way it organises its collective life. Less densely populated countries will fare better. France is a good example of a developed economy that has prepared for the future, and this coupled to her low population density will give her a significant edge.

The longer investment is put off, even allowing for expected improvements in technology, the worse will be the ultimate reckoning.

A hydrogen economy

So what are the long-term options? There is no lack of potential fuel if one is prepared to invest the necessary HMC or take some risks. As we have pointed out, the sun beams down over 10,000 times as much energy as we take from fossil sources. There is a lot of uranium and other fissile material about too, but as in the case of using the sun, the outputs from these are in the form of electricity. One cannot fly planes or fuel ocean liners with long cables attached to land-based electrical generating stations. Nor is there a lot of enthusiasm for converting nuclear submarines into ocean freighters. Quite clearly not everything can be converted to using electricity. So we turn to a proposal that had a huge airing about twenty years ago: the so-called hydrogen economy.

The idea is that hydrogen becomes the fuel of the future. It can be made very easily by hydrolysing water with an electric current. When it burns it produces an innocent waste product – water. Hydrogen can be distributed through the existing natural gas pipeline network as a substitute for natural gas. Cooked up with coal it can manufacture liquid fuels or other hydrocarbon products. So the question is this: can we do all these things on the scale required? And can we do them in time? The answer is 'yes we can' if we are prepared to forgo some of the trivia of our consumer society in the interim.

We explored the potential for a hydrogen economy for the UK, that would be free of the need for fossil fuels. We found it was not going to be easy. The investment requirements were too onerous. This is not because there is a lack of renewable energy potential but because the population density is too high in relation to that potential. It would be achievable only if a lower material standard of living were accepted by the populace. Only by enlarging the UK's nuclear power capacity for some decades could a hydrogen economy finally based on renewable sources become a reality and existing standards of living be maintained.

The prospects are better for those countries with a low population density. In fact the average global population density is one twelfth of that of the UK.

A global hydrogen economy

So what are the prospects at the global level? We shall approach the analysis as a top-down, planned global energy policy,[10] while realising that putting it into practice is outside present possibilities. It is, however, a good way of understanding both the potential and the problems.

As always, implementing such a policy means diverting an enormous amount of capital (HMC) from other sectors of the economy. By way of example we shall adopt a simple rule to guide investment. We shall take a fraction of the physical 'wealth' (i.e. HMC) that we currently derive from fossil fuels and treat it as a 'royalty' to be channelled directly and immediately into renewable energy systems. In this way, as they become operational, consumption of fossil fuels will gradually decrease until, eventually, sufficient new infrastructure has been developed to meet energy demands from renewable sources alone. We draw heavily here on studies made by our one-time colleague, David Crane.

Here is how we implement the policy:

Initially investment in non-fossil electrical generation is made at a rate determined by the rate of depletion of fossil fuels multiplied by a 'royalty'. So with the world depleting oil at a rate of seven billion tonnes per year and a royalty of 4% (for example) the energy invested in building non-fossil electricity generation would be equivalent to 280 million tonnes of oil equivalent per year. Compare this with the present rate of investment where in 1999 some 80 million tonnes were embodied in the capital stock of the electricity supply system, and some 70 million embodied in other energy supply systems like oil rigs, refineries, distribution networks etc. It is important to appreciate that these figures refer only to the investment in *fixed* capital, and do not include the fuel directly consumed by the electricity and fossil fuel supply industries.

As the new technologies gain a foothold, fewer and fewer fossil-fired generators are required. The redundant ones can be shut down. Carbon dioxide pollution begins to fall. When 100% of electricity demand is finally met by renewables, the fossil-fired generating plants are permanently phased out. Thereafter further construction is dedicated to producing hydrogen. For simplicity we do not here consider the conversion of hydrogen to synthetic fuels.

Because the time scale for all this runs into decades, the tests are extended to the year 2100. Two factors play a considerable role in the outcome. They are the pace at which the hydrogen economy is introduced (i.e. the size of the 'royalty'), and the year in which the investment programme begins.

First, let us consider the 'royalty' term. How much of the potential wealth derived each year from fossil fuels should be set aside to create a substitute? In other words how much belt tightening is required?

We experimented with a range of values. Starting with a royalty of 1% we doubled it for each successive test to 2%, 4%, 8% and 16%. We set in motion the development of a hydrogen economy in 1995 (the study was done in 1992). The technologies we chose were a mix of 40% nuclear power, 51% photovoltaics and 9% wind power. We added nuclear power because in an initial exploration we found that renewable energies alone could not do the trick, at least not for the first hundred years, because of the low load factors associated with them – see again Chapter 6.[11]

As one would expect, the higher the royalty the more rapid is the move towards a physically sustainable energy supply, but at a cost of greater belt tightening. Royalties of 8% and 16% even manage a full substitution by hydrogen in the developed world within the time-frame of our study (105 years). After the programme has run for about fifty years more and more of the original equipment becomes worn out so that the annual replacement investment has to be added to those

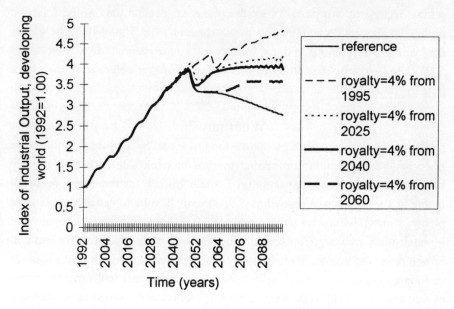

Fig 10.1: Effect of delaying the start-up date for the hydrogen economy for the case of the developing world.

investments, thus expanding the required size of the hydrogen economy. As a consequence industrial output falters. This is partly due to the decision in these trials to sustain investment in social welfare and housing in line with wealth production.

The outlook for the developing world is less encouraging in that attaining a full hydrogen economy is beyond its reach (from its own resources) in the first hundred years, as the diversion of investment (HMC) to renewables saps ability to expand the industrial economy as fast as needed. Nonetheless progress is made and both industrial development and material affluence continue to rise throughout the century. Indeed, in relative terms, the gains are greater than for the developed world, material affluence being 400% higher in 2100 (compared to 1992) when attributing a 4% royalty – the optimum proportion.

Of course none of this is going to happen for some time yet. Governments are institutionally unable to look that far ahead. So what are the consequences of putting off the decision?

It turns out that a late start is still better than doing nothing, which would be disastrous anyway. We ran four substitution tests each with a 4% royalty and starting dates of 1995, 2025 (when oil will start to become scarce), 2040 (when real scarcity looks likely to set in) and 2060 (when natural gas will be in short supply). To our surprise, even putting off a decision till 2060, while it induces a serious recession, can partly offset the persistent decline that would follow if nothing at all were done. However, as may be seen from Figure 10.1, the sooner the hydrogen economy is initiated the less will be the eventual disruption.

We see here a need to think further ahead than ever before in the world of human affairs.

What now?

To sum up, we can indeed escape the limitations set by the world's finite stores of energy, but not without some pain. How are the world's decision makers likely to approach the eventual fossil energy famine? Initially, as at present, they will ignore it. We will be told that with 35 to 60 years of oil and gas in hand there is plenty of time. History, we will be reminded, has shown over and over again that humanity has always circumvented constraints by sheer inventiveness and will power. And who knows, it will be said, what vast hydrocarbon deposits may yet be found, or what remarkable technological developments will serve to reduce energy demand. If this is so, why are some far-seeing companies like BP-Amoco, Sony and Siemens researching and investing with such diligence in renewable energy technologies if not to be ready for the day when they may corner the market? The reader may care to reflect upon the warnings offered by the oil geologist Colin Campbell noted in Chapter 6 that within ten years the Gulf oil states will be the swing oil producers, able to dictate prices.

As for the rebound effect or the tedious limitations imposed by the laws of thermodynamics, these will continue to be politely ignored. Even where the future lies with renewable energies, not every country has enough land area in relation to its population, and many will find the capital cost inhibiting.

Some years ago we explored the interactions of population, area and level of economic development through a methodology entitled national 'potential for change'.[12] It revealed three types of nation state. Those with rising potential, those coasting along, and those with falling potential. This last group were countries already densely populated and with still rising populations, like India, Pakistan and Indonesia. The favoured countries were France, Iceland, Scandinavia, Russia, New Zealand, Australia, Brazil, Chile, Argentina, the USA and Canada. The sad truth is that only rich countries can afford renewable energy systems.

Appendix 3: Natural capital accounting

In a natural capital accounting model such as ECCO, the equations describing the economy are set up in such a way as to express output as the primary energy embodied in the manufacture of goods or the provision of services. (The reader may recall, if she or he has read Appendix 2, that embodied energy is the key element in the relation between money and energy.) Industrial production has three outlets: consumer goods, capital goods or export goods. That portion which is invested (capital goods) is termed Human-Made Capital or HMC. There are two sources of HMC: the manufacturing capacity of the economy and imports.

Physical capital as HMC is absorbed by every sector of the economy both for its maintenance and its expansion. **In an ECCO version of a natural capital accounting model the feedback loops are set up in such a way as to determine what is the potential for growth of the economy if a certain set of policies are pursued**. These models are heavily data-laden, and their construction may well take eight or more person-years of effort even starting with the generic models available off the shelf. As a rule the model is initiated several years back (typically a decade) so that its evolution can be checked against actual national economic performance. This is a process known as validation. Future policies are set by the model user.

The core of these models is a simple positive feedback loop of how the production (or import) of HMC nourishes the manufacturing (industrial) sector. Figure 10.2 illustrates this as an influence diagram – see again Chapter 3.

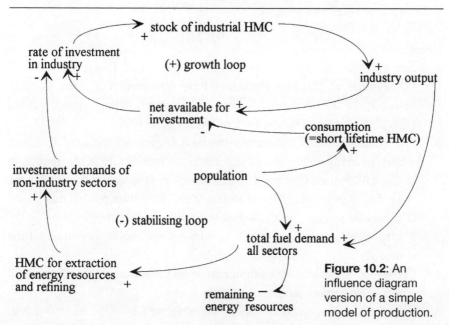

Figure 10.2: An influence diagram version of a simple model of production.

In the figure imports and exports have been omitted for simplicity. The central feedback loop is positive, thus driving growth, which is trimmed by various negative feedbacks, such as the demand for HMC by other sectors of the economy and personal consumption of goods. It must be remembered that virtually any policy proposal and any technology change has implications for energy demand and HMC.

Helping the decision-maker

Since this sort of model is a policy testing tool, human decision-making rests outside the model in the mind of the decision-maker. The model merely tests the outcome of his or her intuition. This is in distinction to econometric models where decision-making is encapsulated in elasticities of demand and supply based upon research outside the model. In judging the outcome of a policy test using an ECCO model (for example as in the European study described in this chapter) the model user has to decide which are the criteria by which s/he will judge the success of a policy. These criteria should be widely spread for, as was seen in the European study, the primary objective of one policy may be fulfilled at the expense of others just as important. Because natural capital accounting models use physical units, they are not subject to the vagaries of money, and so can be extrapolated further into the future than econometric models, and with reasonable confidence.

An interactive ECCO model of the United Kingdom is posted on the world-wide web at www.eccosim.org.uk

Notes

1   Not so little, however, as one might expect. The Lawrence Berkeley Laboratories at Stanford University have estimated that office facilities absorb 2% of the US electricity demand, and that desktop computers in the USA absorbed 14.34 billion kWh of electricity in 1999.

2   The Natural Capital Accounting methodology has been used to create models of many countries and regions under the rubric ECCO – Evolution of Capital Creation Options. The structure of such models is discussed in the book *The Management of Greed* already cited. One such model, that of the UK, may be accessed on the web at www.eccosim.org.uk

3   Not to mention the hard data necessary for the model to crunch all the numbers.

4   These models are relatively simple compared to econometric models, which typically have many thousands of equations.

5   Sustainable Europe Model (SUE), available on CD-ROM from DG XII,

European Commission, Brussels. SUE is an omnibus model of the fifteen EU countries, treated as if they were one single state and economy. However the economy is represented by typical sectors like manufacturing, agriculture, services or transport. Their location is thus not considered. There are eight population age groups, so that it can take account of the demands created by population change.

6   A recent study by the consultants ERM Energy goes so far as to say that to meet the EU's original Kyoto committments on carbon dioxide emissions it will be necessary to build 85 nuclear plants in the next 20 years. See www.europa.int/en/comm/dg17/dilemma.pdf

7   *Modelling Sustainability with PANTA RHEI and SUE*. A. Bockermann, B. Meyer, I.Omann, J.H. Spangenberg, Discussion paper 68 December 2000, Institut für Empirische Wirtschaftsforschung, Universität Osnabruck, D 49069. PANTA RHEI has 40,000 equations. SUE has 2000.

8   GlobEcco – see footnote 14, Chapter 6.

9   This is often denied by economists. But in 1974 we had the privilege of witnessing a massive economic experiment. The oil cartel OPEC unilaterally raised the price of oil threefold. The price of every manufactured product also rose threefold, but the time taken to do so varied between one and five years according to its energy intensity.

10   GlobEcco – see footnote 14, Chapter 6.

11   This study is reported in greater detail in *The Management of Greed*, 1997, M. Slesser, J. King and D. C. Crane , pp152-159.

12   *Potential for Change,* J. Howell and M. Slesser, 1973, Technological Forecasting and Social Change, 5, pp253-264.

11

The world we deserve

Sustainability is a deceptively simple word for an extremely complex idea… (It) wraps economics, ecology, social and personal well-being together in one package. It ties the package up with system dynamics and mails the whole thing decades into the future. No wonder it has a hard time making it on the Main Street.
BELIEVING CASSANDRA, ALAN ATKISSON

We opened this book with the contention that money could not take account of nature's contribution to our welfare. This led to the ineluctable conclusion that sustainability (in the true sense of durability) cannot be assessed in monetary units. In the succeeding chapters we explored the physical determinants of durability. We looked at the risks inherent in failing to protect ourselves from the hurricane of globalisation. We explored some simple but radical solutions for achieving global equity and dealing with the epidemic of affluenza sweeping the industrialised countries. The question we turn to now is: how may we hone the dull edge of present uncertainty into the cutting edge of a new and practicable vision?

Vision

If someone had not dreamt of flying there would never have been aeroplanes. But between the vision and the reality lay many years of research, trial and error, hard work, and risks taken. Vision is a precursor of change, but not the means. It is one thing to understand intellectually the need for durability; quite another to implement it. The lip service paid in the past and still being paid to 'sustainable' development is a monument to that remarkable human characteristic: the ability to rationalise one's actions as being for the best. The reality is that we have barely embarked upon our journey. That's the bad news. The good news is that scientific analysis shows that durability is indeed within our reach. However, as the reader may recall from Chapter 1, we must move from acceleration to deceleration.

There is no reason why we should not manage a seamless transition. Beware, however, of those whose nostrums are couched in monetary units. They can be misleadingly optimistic.[1]

Most of us have encountered prescriptions for a better, safer, equitable, more durable world. They generally convey a moral ethic and leave one humbled but frustrated when they founder on the rocks of physical and psychological reality. That primitive urge of the rational self-optimising individual to possess more and yet more is impatient with such visions. Too many of us are firmly in the grip of today's enticing society of consumer populism, picking, choosing and discarding. As children we are brought up under the onslaught of modern advertising. As adults, driven to survival by the exigencies of a market economy, we often find it pays to keep the head down and look after number one. According to Ian Angell, professor of information systems at the London School of Economics, this is sound advice for the new millennium when *'there will be no sanctity of life; that is an outdated Judaeo-Christian ethic... To be successful we are going to have to be more ruthless with each other'.*

If he is not wrong now, we must make sure he soon is! Such a view of society is surely unacceptable. The solution to humanity's problems lies with humanity. We are in danger of becoming our own greatest enemy as we exchange the old sense of community for the lure of the cafeteria society. Of course, when touched by a visionary writer or a particularly compelling TV documentary on the state of the planet we do see the need for change, and wonder briefly if it may come about. But we observe, perhaps with a touch of nostalgia, that the global economy is outpacing global society. It is hard to resist the lure of ever-increasing material wealth and it seems silly not to cash in while we can. Durability can wait.

Even those of us who accept that the race must be run to save the planet, also know only too well that we do not control the levers of power. Nor, it seems, do our politicians. In their folly, or their greed, they have given away their power to the transnational corporations and the World Trade Organisation. They have done this in many ways, but the most significant of all is by legislating that the corporation be treated as a legal persona in its own right. This has resulted in these commercial entities actually being *more* free than we citizens, for they have access to a level of financial power that most of us cannot aspire to. When it comes to legal contest they are almost bound to win. Here is something our legislators should seriously consider acting on.

Yet the fact is that we, as citizens, could still call the shots if we pulled together. Look how the environmental lobby finally forced governments to take the environment on board. We scuttled the Multilateral Agreement on Investment, which would have greatly extended corporate powers. We may be poorer than corporations but we are in the majority. We simply need to exercise our vote. So it is, theoretically, within our power to alter the way the world is run. But we have to want it.[2] And if we do nothing we will inherit the world we deserve.

Let us be clear about how we shall instruct our politicians. They will need first to take very seriously the question of the economy's long-term potential – in physical terms of course, not monetary. This is a specialist task, requiring the skills offered by scientific, economic and systems disciplines and backed up by data much of which does not yet appear routinely in national and international statistics. Assessing long-term potential is only a first step but an immensely important one since without it we shall lack the essential information.

Durability can be achieved in a number of ways and over different time scales. It involves many trade-offs and therefore many choices. The key to effective policy-making, it goes without saying, is to think in terms of feedback. The complex system that represents an aeroplane enables it to fly only because it is organised around a network of positive and negative feedbacks that terminate in the controls in the pilot's cabin. Our governments must legislate the necessary feedbacks, based on a solid understanding of our social, physical and economic systems and their inter-connections.

Once the true facts about durability are understood and the implications considered by the citizens at large, we will surely find ourselves in a stronger position to cajole our politicians into adopting the appropriate measures.

Legislating the appropriate feedbacks will take time to achieve. Not only that, there will be political risks for those involved. But it can be done. That is the important thing. It can be done in such a way that everyone, small and great, individual consumer or business giant, finds it in his, her or their interest to act in a way that also sustains the environment and the economy.

None of this presupposes a fixed future. No-one can know what promising new scientific inventions lie before us. Nor do we know the scale or distribution of future population growth; and we can only guess at the long-term effect of environmental damage to our agriculture and fisheries, the signs admittedly not being very encouraging. Whatever lies ahead, seeking durability does not mean abandoning business creativity. Turning the hydrogen economy into reality, for example, will open up enormous opportunities for entrepreneurs to fill new niches in the market. What matters is how we manage these innovations. All the wishes, all the rules and regulations in the world will be to no avail if they are not thought of in terms of the total system.

What are the means available for people to enter into a broad exchange of ideas and to influence events? One of the most challenging innovations of our times is the internet. It provides a wealth of opportunity but a host of dangers. On the one hand it has the potential to be a people's world parliament. A topic, once it has caught the imagination, flashes round the globe in hours. How quickly was Monsanto brought to its knees over terminator seeds. The internet may well become the new democracy.

On the other hand the internet is an aggressive tool for directing consumption. Moreover e-commerce is predicated on the notion of an ever-expanding economy. At least that is the expectation of those who raised the price of stocks like Amazon.com and its like to dizzy heights before they had even turned a profit. E-mail and certain aspects of the internet have to a great extent become toys which serve to fill up the time of bored citizens. For the mischievous there is the additional allure of filtering a virus into the system, and for the adventurous the challenge of hacking into the Pentagon. The ease and technical allure of e-mail has resulted in a veritable explosion of trivia. It is forecast that it will expand a hundred-fold in the coming decade. A hundred times as much trivia is still trivia. The danger for society is that it becomes imprisoned, insulated from reality, by a virtual wall of cyberspace. According to the US Congress On-line Project the volume of e-mails reaching US senators had in some cases been 55,000 a month, and 80 million a year for Congress as a whole. Since there are not enough staff to read and process such a volume the result has been that e-mails are now 'routinely ignored'. The report added that 'Rather than enhancing democracy – as so many had hoped – e-mail has heightened tensions and public disgruntlement with Congress'.

However the internet can be a prodigious source of information. But as anyone can set up a web-site and so advertise his or her pennyworth of information, the surfer is faced with having to judge its veracity. There are today 20,000 sites devoted to giving (at a price) medical advice. How do we judge the competence of the counsellors? There is a very great risk that the younger generation will grow up believing anything on the internet and making it their sole resource for information. Information once it gets into the loop tends to be repeated and relayed. Once false information is in the loop it assumes the aura of truth.

Futurists tell us that internet commerce will replace the high street store and the corner shop. And it is already is doing so. However none of this reduces the burden on resources. The goods still have to be made, wrapped, transported and delivered. Food still has to be grown and processed. A great deal of nonsense is talked about the future of the developed countries as knowledge-based economies entirely geared to service activities – taking in each others' washing is a better description. This vision[3] assumes that the production of human-made capital (HMC) will largely take place in countries where wages are low. The arrogance of that assumption would be offensive were it not so patently naive. Even if much of the ownership of capital remains with the currently richer countries, it is inevitable that knowledge and skills also will migrate to the so-called developing world. And with nothing to export, how is the developed world to pay its way? The neo-liberal future forecast by Ian Angell, quoted above, and that of others, is a deception. We innovate, we produce or we perish. Society has always developed and can only develop through increments in knowledge of the processes which drive the economy. But we must beware of confusing the virtual economy with the real. The benefit of new knowledge is to open up new perceptions.

Perceptions of reality

One of our greatest problems is to understand the nature of the real world. In truth, we cannot ever know it with absolute certainty. We can only form a perception of it. Whether by education, training or prejudice we come to share our own perceptions with others. This bolsters our view, and hardens into conviction. The process is like this:

real world ————> perceived world ————> mental model
(unknowable)   (understanding)   (modus operandi)

Everything we do, every decision we take is based on how we view the world. In our day-to-day lives we tend to operate through mental models derived from perception, which serve to automate our actions and intercourse. An example is travelling to work. Once the route is worked out, the mental model takes over. Thereafter we journey on autohelm. We hardly need to question this process when it comes to simple, daily activities. It usually works very well. However when the consideration is as complex as the interaction between the economy and nature or the assessment of durability, the simple mental models of the ideologues can be very dangerous. As we have stressed throughout this book, a perception that is based exclusively on an abstraction like money is bound to be fuzzier than one which takes account of well-established natural laws. Our leaders, however, have risen to power on the basis of out-of-date mental models as firmly stamped on their psyche as the Queen's head on the coin of the realm. These have to be dislodged and up-dated.

Into action

Let us summarise the prerequisites for durability laid bare in the earlier chapters of this book.
*   A durable economy needs a durable flow of energy.
*   Economic activities must be tailored to the capacity of the environment to dissipate the pollution and waste generated.
*   Positive feedback must be balanced by negative feedback.
*   The money system needs modification so as to be our servant, not our master.
    And let us add one other criterion yet to be discussed: the re-integration of society.

These five desiderata raise some enormous problems.

Providing a durable flow of energy as we move out of the fossil era is going to strain our management skills and force us to make some unpalatable decisions. Lack of technology is not the problem.

Moderating global economic activity to match the capacity of the environment will require some major changes in life-style for rich and poor nations alike. This will not be universally popular. It will require substantial investment in environmental science.

Bringing the money system to heel will deprive some people of a great deal of power. History tells us that it is something not readily relinquished. This will be a real test of our leaders!

At first sight it might seem that the task is so great as to be achievable only on a war-time footing. Certainly the scale and nature of the change required cannot be left to the voluntary action of caring individuals, though they will form the troops to man the bridgehead. Nor is it sensible to try to swim against the current. There is nothing so depressing as a lost cause. The approach must be to adapt the existing free market to meet our objectives, and this for the very good reason that it is a system which is innately self-correcting; that is, highly sensitive to negative feedback. But as pointed out in earlier chapters the free market has one serious flaw (among many others). Being expressed in monetary units the feedbacks do not embrace nature's contribution to our welfare. Her role must therefore be determined for every branch of economic activity and from that understanding the appropriate feedbacks legislated.

This will involve a change in economic priorities. Energy-intensive inputs must be made more expensive than formerly, while labour, that is decision-intensive inputs, must be unburdened from taxes. Quite simply, this means raising taxes through energy and reducing them on incomes. The contingent analysis approach of economics, reflecting people's opinions on the monetary value of various aspects of the environment, shows there is an awareness of a need for valuing its contribution, but is far from sufficient. For one thing, the further away in time something is to be evaluated, the less the perceived value will be. When the need to act becomes evident, it may already be too late.

Decision-intensive or resource-intensive?

Bringing nature into the equation also helps to solve another of modern society's bugbears: unemployment. The conventional wisdom is to try and do this through economic growth, but there is a strange paradox here. Competition in a free market economy succeeds by maximising profits. More frequently than not, this is achieved by down-sizing the workforce and increasing capitalisation, resulting in more energy use and fewer jobs per unit output. We are all too familiar with news items reporting job losses as firms seek to become more competitive. Every merger is justified on the grounds of greater efficiency – that is, a smaller workforce. As a result society is becoming divided between the employed, some of whom are inadequately remunerated, who spend too much of their time at work, and the unemployed who have but little involvement in the affairs of the nation. The reader may recall the study on the 'sustainability' of the European Union discussed in Chapter 10 which revealed the sad truth that the economy can never grow fast enough to achieve the goal of full employment without compromising that other objective – durable development.

However if ideas like the global souming (Chapter 8) and personal energy rights (Chapter 9) were in play, then market forces would be quite different. The balance between human labour and energy use would shift in labour's favour. It is as well to remember that every unemployed person represents an unused capacity to deliver human effort and intelligent decision. At the same time every economic action that uses more energy than necessary increases the rate of depletion of the world's energy stores and increases pollution.

If putting an unallocated human resource – someone without a job – to work consumes no additional physical resource, then it increases the sum of human welfare without adding to resource depletion. We can all think of hundreds of ways that people can contribute their time without invoking resources: the grandmother that cares for the grandchildren, the voluntary charity worker, the friendly neighbour.

What this boils down to is that some economic activities are decision-intensive and some resource-intensive. Measured in monetary units this distinction does not surface. It could, however, provide the basis for a new kind of financial decision-making. Let us suppose that there is a desire to expand caring facilities for elderly people in the community and that the conventional way to do it is to raise taxes. Caring is very much a decision-intensive activity. Consider the effect under two regimes: one of conventional labour-based taxation, and one under some form of energy taxation.

By raising taxes both regimes reduce overall disposable income. Part is subsequently restored through the additional income of those caring for the elderly. Under a labour taxation regime their wages will be spent in the usual way, uninfluenced by the energy intensity of the products they buy (energy being so cheap). There is therefore a real imputed resource cost in providing additional carers. Under a unitax regime, the carers will spend their wages with more discretion tending, in the interest of obtaining value for their money, to avoid energy-intensive products.

With present labour taxation systems many of the initiatives people would like to see brought into play are being needlessly squashed on grounds of cost, when in fact the main cost is not for physical, non-renewable resources but to pay for abundant and renewable labour. We are often artificially and needlessly tying our hands behind our backs.

By seeing the distinction between decision-intensive and energy-intensive activities the so-called forthcoming pension crisis fades. The problem as perceived is that the proportion of elderly people to income earners is known to be rising. This is seen as placing an unacceptable burden on active workers whose incomes will have to be taxed more heavily. Remember, however, that it is energy working through HMC that makes things, not people. People manage machines and other people. The productivity of a modern economy rests less on the size of the working population than on the productivity of its machines. The wealth they produce should be for all. Those who work and profit today do so on the shoulders of those now retired. If taxes have to rise, so be it. The opinion expressed in a recent report that Germany's 'ageing' crisis is such that it will need 500,000 immigrant workers to maintain its pensionable population reveals a misunderstanding of the situation.

Local currency units

Another way in which the economy can be moved from energy-intensive to decision-intensive activities is through the concept of local currency units. Sometimes known as LETS – Local Exchange and Trading System – there are, according to Douthwaite,[4] over a thousand of these systems worldwide. LETS can work on two distinct levels, either by the circulation of special currency notes exchangeable only between signed-up members of a LETS organisation, or through a more informal network with someone keeping rigorous accounts. The Swiss Wirtschaftring (Economic Circle), for example, involves a system of internal currency between businesses, and has grown to 60,000 account holders with a turnover of £1.2 billion.

Another example of an informal internal market occurs in Japan[5] where a special currency has been created by 300 non-profit organisations. The unit of account is an *hour of service*. By offering such help units are accumulated. These can be drawn on to the extent that a credit has been built up, say when one grows older and frailer.

In these informal markets a snag arises if someone contributes more than s/he uses, and then wants to cash that credit into national currency. It cannot be done. The credit can only be used for decision-intensive activities. The truth is that as things stand at present the combination of the money system with the labour taxation system artificially deprives the community of its full potential. However when taxation is switched to energy then human time is always untaxed and can be freely deployed.

Reforming the money system

Reform of the money system is as much a matter of attitude as of action. We need to appreciate that money masks what is going on, that it is a veil laid over the physical asset. We have to understand that in making investment decisions, especially in the public sector, a distinction is necessary between decision-intensive and energy-intensive activities. But we cannot expect the individual to make these distinctions. For one thing the information is not there. That is why that information has to be embedded in the price of a good or service, reflecting its embodied energy.

With respect to banks, action is needed to gear the rate of creation of money to the real, physical rate of wealth creation[6] – HMC. Note the emphasis on *rate*. This is not possible if the ability to create credit remains at the discretion of individual banks. One alternative is that money creation should be exercised only by central (government-controlled) banks. Though this is technically possible, the power shift will be strongly resisted. It remains to be seen whether the G-8 leaders who complain so loudly about the world's capital markets, have the toughness necessary to implement such a step. According to Huber[7] only three central banks matter: the US Federal reserve, the European Central Bank and the Bank of Japan.

Adapting the World Trade Organisation

Oddly enough this bogeyman organisation may prove to be the best vehicle for administering decisions at the global level. It is already influential. It has a secretariat in place. It simply needs to recast its objectives along the lines of the global souming, becoming the World Environment and Resource Organisation. In this way environmental, trade and financial correctness could be combined within one entity owing its existence only to its member states. The Organisation is, after all, a creature of our own human making, albeit through the filter of our politicians. In the last resort they must do what we, the people tell them.

An integrated society

Risk is the handmaiden of success. New directions are unlikely to be achieved without it. The explosion of passion in Seattle at the time of the 1999 WTO meeting is a case in point. It has happened again since, notably in Genoa in 2001. Nuclear warheads, too, might still be stored in Greenham Common (whatever one might think of the merits of the case) were it not for some passionate and dedicated women. Nonetheless the body politic today, inflicted by the virus of affluenza, has become more supine. It is inclined to accept the wisdom of authority, confining its protests to the mannerisms of political correctness and indulging in what Edward Luttwark calls the new '*prohibitionism*': 'In the absence of any plausible theory that suggests another course the insecure majority makes no economic demands. It accepts without question the unchallengeable sovereignty of the market and the absolute primacy of economic efficiency over almost any social purpose. Instead it vents its anger and resentment by punishing, restricting and prohibiting all that can be punished, restricted and prohibited'.[8]

This aspect of modern society is exacerbated by the intrusion of mobile computers through which one can access pre-programmed information, thus removing the need to make decisions, such as which route to take from A to B. The latest gimmick is to fit the car with a DVD furnished with a map disk and a satellite navigation device. You are where the spot indicates. Why not go the whole hog, and replace the driver? Even more alarming is the news of an emotionally sensitive computer mouse, which can sense your stress level, and then seek to reduce it by switching on a soothing screen saver! Heaven save us from gadgets that take away our right to control our own emotions.

The encroaching nanny state is counter-productive. It is depriving us of the very self-reliance that is implicit in the true concept of durability. Nothing that has human involvement can be totally free from risk, so there can be no totally safe solutions. Durability, like safety, is a matter of being aware. We can never hope to make the politicians change unless we take a more independent approach.

Physical and economic durability cannot be realised without social cohesion. Communities must be re-integrated. The global village only makes sense if it is a world of many independent villages. In the smaller integrated communities where people know one another, villains and cheats are easily identified and constrained. An integrated community can police itself naturally and with the internet a fact of modern life, such communities are no longer isolated. In such an environment the all-pervading nanny state with its endless stress-inducing regulations is unnecessary. Lee Kuan Yew, who as prime minister lead the colonial relic of Singapore into one of the most vibrant economies and societies in the world, was asked after his retirement how such an ethnically diverse society managed to remain so coherent. In response he said: 'It is much more difficult [today] than 50 years ago to envisage the future because we are moving into an atomised world where physical location no longer implies cohesion for people at that location... The physical obligation to each other because you share the same piece of land will be under great stress because you can opt out. What will happen when the successful opt out and leave the unsuccessful behind?... Somehow adjustments must be made that will enable people to feel an obligation to each other. In the past people have been bonded to each other by having defended a piece of territory and saying 'this is my way of life, this is my language, this is my culture'... We are going to have to grope our way forward and make sure that we don't unscramble some of the basic bindings that have held societies to together for centuries. Let's not be too eager to abandon the old times we might not have something enduring to replace them with....You have to have a hard core (of the populace) who say 'I will make this place work.'. [9]

We leave the last word to the Club of Rome[10] that did so much to alert the world to the problems which now beset us: 'It is necessary for the ship of state to be not only kept afloat, but also steered, surely and deliberately, towards a desired destination'.

Notes

1   For example the book *Natural Capitalism* by A. Lovins A. H. Lovins and P. Hawken, 1999, Little, Brown & Co., Boston.

2   Those who would like to join the struggle should contact the internet site: www.attac.org/suisse/GE

3   For example, that of Dr Madsen Pirie, who directs the Adam Smith Institute.

4   *The Ecology of Money,* R. Douthwaite, 1999, Schumacher Society briefing no. 4.

5   Bernard Lietaer describes this in a foreword to Richard Douthwaite's *The Ecology of Money.* A special currency called Hureai Kippu (caring relationship tickets) has been created by 300 groups of non-profit organisations.

6   What is wealth and wealth creation is a vexed question, especially amongst environmentalists and ecologists. However, drawing on the natural capital accounting approach discussed in Chapter 5, wealth creation is definable as the human made capital (HMC) that can be harnessed to production.

7   For a useful exposition on this technically complex subject see *Plain Money,* J. Huber,1999, Institut für Soziologie, Abderhaldenstr. 7, Germany 06099 or www.soziologie.uni-halle.de/publikationen/index.html

8   *Turbo Capitalism: Winners and Losers in the Global Economy*, E. Luttwak, 1998, Weidenfeld and Nicolson.

9   An interview with Lee Kuan Yew reported in *New Perspectives Quarterly*, Blackwell, summer 1999, p22.

10   *The First Global Revolution,* A. King and B. Schneider, 1991, Simon & Schuster, London. Also published in several other languages.

Epilogue

The good life is one of endeavour, achievement and contentment. It sustains our natural instinct to probe the frontiers of knowledge and technology and to make the best of our lives. What, then, if we embrace the idea of a non-accelerating economy with the aim of attaining a measure of durability? To many such a prospect must frankly seem at best a recipe for boredom and at worst an economic disaster. Think again. The joys of the affluent society may be many, it is true, but the virus of affluenza has weakened our metabolism and we are behaving as if tomorrow had been cancelled. In our heart of hearts we know things cannot go on as they are.

Any move towards durability will call for all the imagination, creativity and investment we can muster. This will mean neither a stagnant society, nor a stagnant economy. Far from it. The task just of creating a viable economic system that is no longer dependent on fossil fuels will be a major challenge, calling for innovation in virtually every field. New technologies of energy transfer and fresh applications of motive power will have to be found. Emphasis on minimising resource use and reducing waste will demand new ways of thinking and behaving both for commerce and the individual citizen. Giving a leg up to the poorer countries will call for new forms of global co-operation. Rethinking globalisation and working out the transition to durability will require all the social, political and diplomatic skills we can assemble. The new mentality could permeate everywhere, reinvigorating a society all too frequently skewed to consumerism and passive entertainment. At the same time, with money as the flux of the economy, GDP can still increase. Market mechanisms will remain, but within a framework of intelligent constraint. Wall Street may take the view that happiness cannot make money, but let us remind ourselves of Alice Walker's words: *if your chain is gold, so much the worse for you.*

The individual is central to this transformation. Governments like to please us, so influencing them through our votes is the key to durability. This is why it is essential that there be the widest possible understanding of the facts amongst the population. When understanding is lacking people tend to fall back on assumptions and become a prey to ideologues and not-so-scrupulous politicians. We have a responsibility to be clear about what needs to be done and how it may affect our daily lives. It is only when the majority accepts the need for a transition that it will come about.

The push for change has to come first from those of us who understand the need for it. That is why a key purpose of this book has been to make the underlying features of a durable economy understandable to any intelligent citizen willing to take the time to appraise them, emphasising that the burden of interpretation must not be left to monetary analysis alone. To secure the bridgehead to the future we shall need the idealists (but not the ideologues). However we cannot rely on selfless, voluntary action alone. We need the pragmatists who realise that the status quo is not an option. The pathway to successful change, as we have tried to demonstrate, is through policies built on an understanding of the principle of feedback. People cannot be expected to act in ways compatible with a durable future if it does not coincide with their own personal interests. The answer is to introduce strategies which ensure that in the day-to-day dealings of life, the interests of individuals and of society coincide.

Consider one example of where the right feedbacks are missing: food provision. Each of us acting in our personal role as *Homo economicus* tends to seek the best value for our money. The arena is the supermarket. The positive feedback from this is that supermarkets pressure the farmers who are forced to compete with cheap imports. This leads to many unholy practices: recycled animal remains, battery farming and excessive artificial fertilisation of soils. The intensification of agriculture in pursuit of profit and competitiveness has led to ever greater risks of animal and human disease and dire consequences for the agricultural community. Globalisation of trade has increased the risks even further. The villain, we can say, is greed, and its handmaiden trade. The solution is to legislate the appropriate negative feedbacks. If they are not obvious then we have to seek them out.

As we saw in Chapter 10, we cannot have our cake and eat it too. The environment and durability are not separate issues. They are inextricably linked. This does not make the problems insoluble, but it does require that they be dealt with holistically. There is little point in economic growth that does not deliver durability. Once the trade-offs are recognised difficult choices may have to be made. For example, it is hard to see how the energy-intensive life-style of the average European or American can be maintained without recourse to nuclear energy, at least in this century. Unless we opt for a much less opulent life-style it may well be that we find ourselves going back to burning coal in conjunction with carbon dioxide absorption techniques, expensive though that would be.

As an appreciation of the virtues of the new order penetrates, the way will be open for innovation on a grand scale. Those companies that have anticipated the changing scene will have the competitive edge. The opportunities are legion, from pollution control to exploiting energy from the oceans, or to producing less resource-intensive packaging. Manufacturers will have an even greater incentive than today to improve product design and production in accordance with the new ethic. Energy rather than labour productivity will be what counts. Emphasis will change to product durability, potential for easy repair and recycling. Volkswagen is already leading the way.

The conventional worry is that if an economy is no longer accelerating (even though evolving) massive unemployment will arise. This need not be so if we switch from labour taxation to energy as discussed in Chapter 9. Then all sorts of possibilities open out, particularly where socially useful work is sorely needed but deemed 'uneconomical' under today's tax systems. The conditions for full employment become a tangible reality. An analysis made by Michael Renner in a Worldwatch paper of September 2000 gives a rather hopeful view of the employment situation in a more environmentally concerned world.

With a range of new employment opportunities opening up, and in a society which could turn out to have fundamentally different ways of doing things, the educational system will surely have to be reassessed radically. Perhaps we will decide to go back to an earlier dream where work, education and leisure were linked together as a single process throughout a person's life. This, however, as with many other aspects of the transition to the durable economy, is a subject for a different book.

What of the stock market, that bell-weather of economic stability? How can it sustain a decelerating economy? Well, it depends on what is decelerating; hopefully it will be the exploitation of depletable resources as well as pointless kinds of trade like transporting potatoes far away simply to have them washed more cheaply before bringing them all the way back again. Clearly those companies that are highly geared or who exist simply by buying and selling the output of others are at greatest risk of a drop in their share price. Even here, though, one must distinguish between new technology that is productive, like photovoltaic systems for collecting energy from the sun, and the production of consumer trivia. The shrewd investor need have no fears.

Investment is not simply something done through the stock market. It can also take the form of measures to reduce one's own living costs. For example when does it make sense to buy a really energy-efficient car like the Toyota Prius or a condensing boiler (furnace) for one's central heating? The Prius costs about £4000 more than a normal car. That extra money could buy an awful lot of fuel at today's prices, so fuel prices have to change dramatically before the individual can benefit from such an investment. For the same reason there is currently little financial incentive to switch to a more fuel-efficient condensing boiler . It is a government's business to legislate the conditions that make such investments desirable from an individual's point of view. But what could be more exciting for the family than to be linked to the internet through a computer powered by one's own solar energy source?

Information on such things is not available to the general consumer, but it should be, and hopefully will be in time. In the case of both nations and individuals, although some may be instinctively astute enough to be ahead of the game, the information for making decisions in the interest of durability can really be gained only by taking a long-term view of the situation, supported by physical econometric dynamic analysis.. This will tell one when the artificial inflation of the money-driven economy will be constrained by physical reality. Even as we write the first signs are showing up in the USA.

At the moment, in the more developed countries, the rate of reduction in energy use through efficiency measures is not enough to compensate for the annual increase in energy use overall due to economic acceleration. Moreover the prospects for making efficiency improvements are finite. There is another factor too to take account of. It requires energy to make the materials that make possible the reduction in energy use. In the long run the availability of energy is limited by natural physical principles – the second law of thermodynamics – although there is still a long way to go. The astute investor will have foreseen this situation.

The coming transition will, like any other, have its problems and challenges. The terrorist attack on the World Trade Center on 11 September 2001 has irrevocably changed the world. It also brought a sharp correction to the stock market, one that would in any case have happened sooner or later though without such grief and loss of life. It certainly has diluted the civil liberties of the citizens of the western democracies. That is bad news. At the same time immense scope is offered for change, whether for the inventor, the innovator, the investor or the ordinary citizen. Life in the new society will be far from boring. Let's go for it now!

Index